ACKNOWLEDGMENTS

A Family Perspective in Church and Society was prepared under the aegis of the Bishops' Ad Hoc Committee on Marriage and Family Life, Bishop Howard Hubbard, chairman. Other bishop members of the committee who contributed considerable time and effort were Bishops John Snyder, Joseph Sullivan, Dale Melczek, Eugene Marino, Joseph Delaney, and John Ricard.

The actual preparation of this manual took place over a four-year period and required five major drafts. The manual was developed through an extensive process of consultations involving the committee, the writers, consultants, diocesan representatives, national organizations, and marriage and family life movements.

Its principal writers were Revs. Thomas Lynch and Steven Preister. Major assistance was also given by Rev. David O'Rourke, Sr. Faith Mauro, and Ms. Theodora Ooms.

Grateful appreciation is offered to the presidents and members of the National Association of Catholic Diocesan Family Life Ministers for their contribution in the formulation of the vision contained in this manual. The Presidents were Revs. Thomas Boland, John Bishop, and Peter Casey. The Association provided critical and systematic feedback on each draft of the manual.

The development of this manual was a collaborative effort of the members of the Ad Hoc Committee on Marriage and Family Life. These members consulted with the organizations and networks that they represented so that their concerns and those of hundreds of men and women readers were addressed by the writers and incorporated in the text. The members of the Ad Hoc Committee were Sharon Daly, Rosemary Salazar, Mary Lynch Barnds, Valerie Dillon, Lawrence Rilla, Chuck Ryan, Mary Pat Mulligan, Thomas Martin, Ronald Sharps, Mary Jo Czaplewski, Richard and Barbara McBride, Dolores Leckey, Robert and Diane Nicholson, Betsy Redgate, John Farnsworth, Kathy and Jim McGinnis; Srs. Teresa Barchie, Rita Baum, Angelita Fenker, Faith Mauro; and the Revs. Joseph Kenna, Thomas Boland, John Bishop, Peter Casey, Edward Bryce, Joseph DiMauro, Joseph Fenton, James McHugh, James Gill, Joseph Cavoto, and John Zietler.

A
FAMILY
PERSPECTIVE
IN
CHURCH AND
SOCIETY

A
MANUAL
FOR
ALL
PASTORAL
LEADERS

Ad Hoc Committee on Marriage and Family Life
National Conference of Catholic Bishops

At its September 1987 meeting, the Administrative Committee of the National Conference of Catholic Bishops approved *A Family Perspective in Church and Society: A Manual for All Pastoral Leaders*, a statement of the NCCB Ad Hoc Committee on Marriage and Family Life. The following text has been reviewed and approved by the Most Reverend Howard Hubbard, Chairman of the Ad Hoc Committee on Marriage and Family Life, and is authorized for publication by the undersigned.

Monsignor Daniel F. Hoye
General Secretary
December 4, 1987   NCCB/USCC

Cover Design: Rabil and Associates; Gaithersburg, Md.

Typography: World Composition Services, Inc.; Leesburg, Va.

Typeface: Palatino

ISBN 1-55586-191-1

CONTENTS

FOREWORD AND NOTE TO READERS

The American family is at a crossroads. Empirical studies corroborate the evidence we see daily in homes, neighborhoods, and the media—family life today is facing change and is under tremendous societal pressures. In the face of these challenges, the family almost single-handedly has responded with astounding strength and staying power. However, the family need not and should not stand alone.

The Church has historically been an advocate of strong family life. This manual builds on this history, urging the Church and its leaders to take strong and immediate action by incorporating a *family perspective* in all its policies, programs, ministries, and services.

The Church possesses the resources to support and act as an advocate for families. The Church's theology provides a strong foundation and assurance; the Church's presence and moral power must be tapped. The state of the family has been verified; the need is clear; the direction has been set; immediate action is possible. The Catholic Church in the United States can be informed, alerted, and empowered to place the family at the center of its work and worship. The Church can join hands with all social institutions and all people of good will who daily see the results of beleaguered and undersupported families.

This manual explains what a family perspective is, and its basic elements. It describes the implications of a family perspective for Church and social leaders and proposes some creative ways for implementing a family perspective in Church and society's policies, programs, ministries, and services. It is not intended to be a treatise on family life, although it draws on theology, Catholic tradition, and the sciences expli-

cating family life. Rather, it is intended to provoke continuing pastoral action in support of family life.

This manual is the result of a decade of careful listening to families, study, and discussion. In 1978, the Catholic bishops of the United States adopted *The Plan of Pastoral Action for Family Ministry: A Vision and Strategy*. As a result, dioceses across the nation have become more pro-active in developing programs for marriage and family life. The Church's interest has also paralleled the concern of other Churches and government (e.g., the National Council of Church's Committee on Family Ministry; the White House Conference on Families; and activities of the U.S. House of Representatives, for example, the Committee on Children, Youth, and Families).

This manual is written by the NCCB Ad Hoc Committee on Marriage and Family Life because of its responsibility to oversee the implementation of *The Plan of Pastoral Action for Family Ministry* and Pope John Paul II's papal exhortation on the family, *Familiaris Consortio*. As important as the *Plan* is, the committee, challenged by the papal exhortation, became convinced that implementing a family perspective in the Church's policies, programs, ministries, and services is the next needed and logical step in the development of family ministry.

The committee does not believe that family life is facing its demise; the committee does believe that aspects of family life are changing. Many Americans do not recognize the nature or the implications of these changes and are, therefore, unprepared to face them. This manual seeks to equip leaders and institutions with the necessary data and direction to promote the well-being of family life into the twenty-first century.

This manual is addressed to national, diocesan, and local church leaders in the various ministries of the Church who directly or indirectly minister to families. (The term "church leaders" includes bishops, pastors, priests, deacons, religious, ministers, professional staff, lay leaders, and volunteers). This manual is also directed to leaders in social institutions, with the hope of engaging them in a meaningful dialogue so that their policies, programs, and services can be more supportive of marriage and family life. It is also our hope that this manual will promote a greater collaborative partnership with other ecumenical and interfaith communities to support family life.

The manual has been developed to help interested persons apply the elements of a family perspective to their policies, programs, ministries, and services. The committee realizes how difficult it will be to refocus one's thinking from an individual-centered approach to a family-centered approach. Therefore, it is our hope that leaders will convene the appropriate persons in their national, diocesan, and parish offices. The purpose would be to read, study, and reflect on this manual so that the concept of a family perspective will have practical implications.

The manual is also designed to help readers deepen their understanding of a family perspective and its

1

elements. Accordingly, the manual and companion materials are organized into four parts:

- *Level One* is a broad introduction to a family perspective. Chapter One overviews family life today, and Chapter Two briefly describes the four elements of a family perspective; it also contains *leadership implications*, which will help readers think about the relationship between ministry and family life. Chapter Three focuses on implementing a family perspective.
- *Level Two* presents a deeper understanding of the four elements of a family perspective (Chapters Four through Seven). The *Family Impact Questions* found at the end of each of these chapters will assist readers as they work to incorporate a family perspective in their policies, programs, ministries, and services.
- *A Reading Guide* is offered near the end of this manual for interested persons to continue to develop their understanding of a family perspective. It consists of a short reading list, followed by a comprehensive listing of references and readings.

- *Practical Resources for Implementing a Family Perspective*—still in preparation—are described at the end of this manual. *A Family Perspective Resource Book* will be developed by the writers of this manual as a companion resource. This companion resource also will include practical tools for implementing a family perspective in parishes.

Finally, the National Association of Catholic Diocesan Family Life Ministers has formed a committee to develop strategies and materials that will facilitate the incorporation of a family perspective within the Church. The committee also encourages organizations, dioceses, parishes, and movements to develop their own practical tools to assist in incorporating a family perspective in their policies, programs, ministries, and services.

Most Reverend Howard J. Hubbard
Chairman, Ad Hoc Committee on
Marriage and Family Life
National Conference of Catholic Bishops

Level One
An Introduction to a Family Perspective

Level One is a broad introduction to a family perspective:

- *Chapter One* overviews family life today.
- *Chapter Two* briefly describes the four elements of a family perspective; it also contains *leadership implications* that will help readers think about the relationship between ministry and family life.
- *Chapter Three* focuses on implementing a family perspective.

CHAPTER ONE
PURPOSE OF THIS
MANUAL

Introduction[1]

Today the American family stands at a crossroads and faces fundamental challenges. It is society itself that brings to the family great pressures and great opportunities. Among the opportunities that are signs of hope for today's families, the following must be noted:

- From the time of the American Revolution, the story of the American family is characterized by persistent change, but we know that many of these changes have accelerated over the past generation. Since the Revolution, families in America have lived through the most intense and compacted period of social change in the history of civilization. As we moved from an agricultural to an industrial to a technological society, families have adjusted; experts agree that the families are here to stay.[2]
- Americans strongly believe in marriage and family life. Not only are we among the most marrying people in the world, but every pertinent public opinion poll indicates that the majority of Americans consider marriage and family life to be the most important part of their lives.[3]
- People across the nation have expressed a growing interest in marriage enrichment, parenting education, natural family planning, and the rediscovery of family spirituality. One specific example is the church-sponsored process of marriage preparation involving hundreds of thousands of engaged and married couples who witness to the joys and struggles of marriage.[4]
- Because the majority of women are in the work force today, men and women are sharing more of the responsibilities of parenting, and fathers' and mothers' roles have become more flexible. Fathers who live with their children appear to be more involved with them.
- Many service institutions are showing a renewed interest in family life and how to provide their services in ways that support families' own responsibilities. For example, health care institutions over the last years have made notable innovations, such as hospices for dying persons and opportunities for family participation in birthing.
- In the public arena, conservatives and liberals are moving toward the consensus that family concerns should be front and center of the public policy-making process.[5] For the first time, policymakers are talking about injecting a family perspective into public policy and human services.
- During the past two decades information about the natural methods of family planning has become more effectively circulated. The reliability of the various methods has been scientifically supported, and instructional techniques have been constantly defined. The number of couples successfully using the natural methods is constantly growing.

However, there are other changes in society that present both challenging opportunities as well as dangers for many families:

- In 1985, 7% of the nation's families lived in the so-called traditional arrangement: a working father, a stay-at-home mother, and one or more children. Forty-eight percent of mothers with infants under one year of age work outside the home at least part time. This rises to over 70% for mothers of school-age children. Twenty-five million children, over half of them with married parents, are in families where the mother is regularly absent from the home for part of the workday. The issue here is not women's employment, but how to balance work and family

---

[1] Any family trends and statistics listed in this *Introduction* where citations are not provided are taken from S. Preister, "Contemporary American Families: Facts and Fables" (Washington, D.C.: The National Center for Family Studies at The Catholic University of America, 1985); and S. Preister, "Marriage, Divorce, and Remarriage in the United States, and Application to American Catholics" in *Catholic Remarriage: Pastoral Issues and Preparation Models* (Mahwah, N.J.: Paulist Press, 1986).

[2] M. J. Bane, *Here to Stay: American Families in the Twentieth Century* (New York: Basic Books, 1976).

[3] G. Gallup, *American Families—1980* (Princeton, N.J.: The Gallup Organization, 1980); and G. Gallup, "Attitudes of the U.S. Public toward Marriage and the Family," Testimony before U.S. Senate Subcommittee, 1983.

[4] D. O'Rourke, et al., *Preparing for Marriage: A Study of Marriage Preparations in American Catholic Dioceses* (St. Meinrad, Ind.: Abbey Press, 1983).

[5] Coalition of Family Organizations, *COFO Memo* Newsletter (Washington, D.C.: American Association for Marriage and Family Therapy, December 1986): 1ff.

life while ensuring that children's well-being is protected. This is an issue that affects the great majority of Americans at some time in their lives and cuts across all economic, gender, religious, racial, and political groups.

- Because women are employed outside the home, the vast majority of families today are required to negotiate and adjust roles and family responsibilities within the home. The previous generation clearly defined the roles of wife and husband, mother and father. Today, each family must define these roles and responsibilities for itself. While this can be seen as an opportunity, it is also a serious source of stress for many families.
- The four-generation family is now the norm in the United States, and the five-generation family is also common. As average life expectancy rises, almost every family today must care for frail elderly members even when, as is often the case, they do not live together. This new phenomenon particularly burdens families where the only parent or both parents work outside the home. Millions of families experience the stresses of these responsibilities and the financial worries for care of family dependents, both young and old.
- A generation ago, the full-time homemaker managed the relationships between the family and the available service institutions. Today, many responsibilities that were once the exclusive domain of the family are now shared with these institutions. Often, people unquestioningly rely on the expert or on specialized services. Families report that their relationships with the education, health, mental health, social service, employment, and legal systems are frequently complex and often stress-filled.
- In previous generations, most Catholics married other Catholics. Today, 17% of Catholics are married to non-Catholics. Further analysis reveals a striking ecumenical development: the lowest percentage of ecumenical marriages, 14%, is found in Catholics over age fifty, but for couples in their forties, thirties, and twenties, the percentage rises to 16%, 21%, and 28% respectively. Today's couples are entering ecumenical marriages at a rate twice that of their parents.[6] In some parts of the country, over half of all marriages involving Catholics are ecumenical. This situation presents some unique opportunities for these families, such as finding their "unity in the sphere of moral and spiritual values," as well as "the contribution they can make to the ecumenical movement."[7] However, there is also a danger present. Ecumenical couples' marriages can weaken if they lack a mutually shared religious vision and a set of moral principles that guide their life together.[8] Conflict over religious issues and practices, especially related to children, can damage family stability. (Note: the canonical term for ecumenical marriage is *mixed marriage*).
- Increased availability of housing since the 1920s and the pervasive spread of privacy as a value have led to the phasing out of boarding and lodging, except among black families and singles. Since the 1920s, the practice of boarding and lodging has been replaced by solitary living. The solitary residence of individuals—almost nonexistent in the nineteenth century—began to increase in the post-World War II period and has further increased dramatically since the 1950s. Sadly, a high percentage of those living alone are elderly widows whose living arrangement is not a matter of choice, but rather, is often an unbearable arrangement.[9] Between 1970 and 1980 there was a 64% increase in persons living alone.
- Between 1970 and 1980, about 50% of Americans changed residences. While most of these moves were not from one part of the country to another, even moving to another location in the same city can change and disrupt a family's relationships with their family of origin, friends, and supportive community services.

But most seriously, a dark picture emerges today that questions whether our society's stated belief in family life is mere lip service:

- The rising divorce rate of the late 1960s and 1970s is well publicized, but few people realize how far back the trend began. In fact, the annual rate of divorce has been rising since 1860, when the U.S. Census began tracking marriage statistics. It has increased 700% since the turn of the century. Although the rate fell during the early years of the Depression, it rose dramatically after World War II. The period from 1950 to the mid-1960s was exceptional in that the annual rates were lower than might be expected, based on the long-term rise of the previous decades. Beginning in 1965, the divorce rates again rose rapidly, reaching a peak in the period from 1979-1981. It appears that the rapid rise is over, at least for the present. The number of divorces in the United States declined in 1982 and 1983, following twenty years of increase. However, the divorce rates increased slightly again in 1984. If recent rates continue, at least one out of three first marriages entered this year will end in divorce. If remarriages are included, which are now failing at a slightly higher rate than first marriages, one out of two marriages begun this year will end in divorce.

[6] J. P. Dolan and D. C. Leege, *A Profile of American Catholic Parishes and Parishioners: 1820s to the 1980s* (University of Notre Dame: Notre Dame Study of Catholic Parish Life, 1985), rpt. no. 2.

[7] John Paul II, *Familiaris Consortio*, Apostolic Exhortation *On the Family* (Washington, D.C.: USCC Office of Publishing and Promotion Services, 1981), 78.

[8] D. R. Hoge and K. Ferry, *Empirical Research on Interfaith Marriage in America* (Washington, D.C.: United States Catholic Conference, 1981).

[9] T. Haraven, *The Diversity and Strength of American Families*, Testimony before the U.S. House of Representatives' Select Committee on Children, Youth, and Families (Washington, D.C.: U.S. Government Printing Office, 1986), 33.

- According to one study, 50% of children of divorced parents have not seen the nonresidential parent for more than a year. Only one child out of every six has some form of regular, weekly contact with his or her father following divorce. Ten years after a divorce, 74% of children never see the noncustodial parent.[10] About 25% of U.S. children now live in a single-parent household, due to separation, divorce, out-of-wedlock births, and the death of a parent; more than 60% will do so before they finish high school. A major problem for single-parent households, which needs to be addressed, is an economic one. Most of these households are female-headed, with little or no financial or emotional support from the fathers of the children. Over 90% of divorcing women take custody of children, yet they lose 73% of their income, while men's income improves by 42% after divorce. Child-support payments constitute less than 10% of total family income for approximately half of the recipients. At least 25% of the fathers ordered to make support payments never make a single court-ordered payment.[11] Thus, millions of children and their mothers fall below the poverty line, leading to what some have called the "feminization of poverty."
- One out of four of this nation's preschool children is living in poverty. One-third of all children will be on some form of public assistance before age eighteen.[12]
- One out of every five babies is now born out of wedlock, 50% more than a decade ago. The majority of these births are by women beyond their teens; in the thirteen largest U.S. cities, out-of-wedlock births now exceed births to married women. For the large majority of these children, legal paternity is never established.
- By 1995, the combined total of single-parent and remarried families will exceed the number of never-divorced two-parent families in the United States.
- The practice of abortion and its concomitant ideology of the "wanted child" constitute a threat to the family as a life-nurturing institution. The destructive effects of abortion on the family have been multiplied by the way in which the family is explicitly treated in recent court rulings on abortion. The family is seen primarily as a grouping of separate individuals or as the delegated agent of the state. In treating family structures merely as restrictions on the rights of private individuals, the Supreme Court has ignored the family's vital role in promoting and protecting these rights.

- Between 1970 and 1980, there was a 157% increase in unmarried persons living together. Most of these situations follow divorce and preceed remarriage.
- Two million children qualify as battered, and the increase of other forms of family violence (spouse, elderly) is documented. Twenty million children live with an alcoholic parent. One million children run away each year, many of them supporting themselves by prostitution. One out of nine youths will be arrested before the age of eighteen. The suicide rate among fifteen- to nineteen-year-olds has tripled in less than twenty years. The use of drugs and alcohol by teenagers, as well as involvement in premarital sex, has been documented.

The committee believes that at least four reasons account for these new opportunities and pressures on families.

First, in the midst of the great family diversity in our nation, families can experience difficulty identifying their vision of family life. They frequently feel confused about their purpose and their responsibilities (see Chapter Four).

Second, our society pays attention to the needs and rights of individuals, but not of family systems (see Chapter Five). Policymakers, human service providers, and employers think in terms of individuals, not of families. For example, there is a tendency for employers to ignore important aspects of the family life of their employees; too often, a single person, a parent of one child, a parent of five children, and an adult caring for a chronically ill elderly parent are treated the same by an employer. These family needs raise such issues as flex-time, utilization of personal sick leave when caring for an ill family member, and the need to attend periodically meetings and consultations, such as school conferences. Policymakers, human service providers, and employers are not cognizant enough of individuals' larger family systems. Such an orientation fragments individuals' lives into segmented compartments—work, family, friends—and makes relationships stressful.[13] This orientation also creates an overemphasis on individualism, which can lead to an obsessive need for self-fulfillment at the expense of others.[14] The body of Western law known as family law, which provided families and family members with supports such as financial aid and exemptions, and which supported family relationships, is being dismantled bit by bit in favor of legal views that emphasize individual concerns.[15]

Third, our society has not, by and large, adjusted to the cultural, ethnic, and structural diversities families have to face today (see Chapter Six). Family life is so fundamental to our way of life that society takes

[10] F. F. Furstenberg and C. W. Nord, "Parenting Apart: Patterns of Childrearing after Marital Disruption" in *Journal of Marriage and Family* 47:4 (November 1985): 893-904.

[11] L. Weitzman, "The Economics of Divorce: Social and Economic Consequences of Property, Alimony and Child Support Awards" in *UCLA Law Review* (August 1981); and L. Weitzman, *The Marriage Contract* (New York: Free Press, 1981).

[12] D. P. Moynihan, *Family and Nation* (New York: Harcourt Brace Jovanovich, 1986).

[13] R. N. Bellah et al., *Habits of the Heart: Individualism and Commitment in American Life* (Berkeley: University of California Press, 1985), 43.

[14] D. Yankelovich, *New Rules: Searching for Self-Fulfillment in a World Turned Upside Down* (New York: Random House, 1981), 3.

[15] J. Noonan, "The Family and the Supreme Court" in *The Catholic University of America Law Review* (Winter 1973): John XXIII Lecture.

for granted that families will be able to handle the pressures that these diversities place on them. Therefore, society often does not provide the resources and support necessary for families' growth and development. In many cases, society ends up complicating the life of the family and adding further pressure.

Fourth, the locus of family responsibility has shifted (see Chapter Seven). American society has fundamentally changed from a family-centered support system to an individual-centered service and information society. This change has, in turn, allowed social institutions to continue to assume many of the family's traditional roles, such as parenting, educating, and providing care. Today, families and social institutions *share* important responsibilities for the needs of individuals. As yet, however, families and social institutions have not found many effective ways to work as partners in meeting those needs.

Rationale

Whether one believes that families are under seige or stress or that they face unique opportunities, the pressures on family life are creating crises that must be met.

Where is the Church in this critical time, and what is its role? In fundamental ways, the Church's place and role must be the same now as in every age. The Church's place is in the world, as an active participant. Its role is to bring the light of the Gospel to the contemporary situation, enabling people to see how God's plan can be lived out here and now. Such is the principle that has guided the preparation of this manual.

To involve itself in the contemporary situation, the Church needs, first of all, to reflect on its own vision of family life (see Chapter Four). The Second Vatican Council and Pope John Paul II have articulated an understanding of family in which the family is the *basic foundation* of the Church and of society, the most basic of all human communities. However, since this understanding has become part of common parlance, people tend to assume that this understanding is only an idealized principle to be held versus a reality to be lived.

After reflecting on and recommitting itself to family life, the Church needs to take a second step of extending its hospitality to all kinds of families. The Church needs to invite all to hear the Good News and to *listen* with open heart and open mind to families as they struggle with the complexities of today's living.

The Church's third step is action. Christians cannot take a value-neutral stance regarding the opportunities and dangers families face today. The Church needs to challenge negative trends and address issues that undermine family strengths. The Church needs to support positive developments, to look for new ways to help families, and to unearth the resources that enable families to move from crisis to growth, from stress to strength. This can be done by incorporating a *family perspective*, as a pastoral strategy, in all its policies, programs, ministries, and services. The Church needs to do this—not because families are in trouble, but because family life is so important in itself and needs the ongoing support of the Church. Family life is fundamental to the healthy life of the Church and society.

CHAPTER TWO
WHAT IS MEANT BY A FAMILY PERSPECTIVE

Using a family perspective in planning, implementing, and evaluating policies, programs, ministries, and services means two things:

1. Viewing individuals in the context of their family relationships and their other social relationships.

As a systems orientation, a family perspective is a lens that focuses on the interaction between individuals, their families, and social situations. For example, rather than seeing a frail elderly person as an isolated individual who needs help, a family perspective assesses what kinds of supportive relationships that person has (or lacks) from family, friends, church, or neighborhood institutions.

2. Using family relationships as a criterion to assess the impact of the Church's and society's policies, programs, ministries, and services.

As a criterion to assess ministry, a family perspective provides a means to examine and adjust systematically policies, program design, and service delivery. Its goal is to incorporate a sensitivity to families and to promote the partnership, strengths, and resources of participating families. A family perspective in ministry does not mean establishing another church office or a new level of bureaucracy to carry out such evaluation. However, it does mean calling all ministries to undertake this critical process.

A family perspective is rooted in the challenge of Pope John Paul II as stated in *Familiaris Consortio*: "No plan of organized pastoral work at any level must ever fail to take into consideration the pastoral area of the family."[1]

At the foundation of a family perspective are *four elements* that touch the very heart of contemporary family life. Bringing a family perspective to bear in ministry means keeping these four elements in mind when planning, implementing, and evaluating policies, programs, ministries, and services.

The First Element: A Christian Vision of Family Life

The family has a unique identity and mission that permeate its tasks and responsibilities (see Chapter Four for a fuller explication).

The Church has a Christian vision of family life, rooted in Scripture and its tradition, which it holds for its own members. The Church also seeks to offer this vision to the larger community of persons and institutions that hold other visions.

Drawing on *Familiaris Consortio* and Catholic tradition, the committee offers this vision and definition of family life: The family is an intimate community of persons bound together by blood, marriage, or adoption, for the whole of life. In our Catholic tradition, the family proceeds from marriage—an intimate, exclusive, permanent, and faithful partnership of husband and wife.

This vision is rooted in the covenantal love of Jesus Christ. It holds that the family "constitutes a special revelation and realization of ecclesial communion, and for this reason too, [the family] can and should be called the domestic church."[2] This vision proclaims that family life is sacred and that family activities are holy. It also proposes a unique family mission. It places the family at the service of building up God's Kingdom in history.[3] This mission also calls families to protect and reveal their intimate community of life and love.

This vision and mission, in turn, empower families to undertake four specific tasks for the good of the Church and society:

1. The family is to form an intimate community of persons.
2. The family is to serve life in its transmission, both physically by bringing children into the world, and spiritually by handing on values and traditions as well as developing the potential of each member to serve life at every age.
3. The family is to participate in the development of society by becoming a community of social training and hospitality, as well as a community of political involvement and activity.
4. The family is to share in the life and mission of the Church by becoming a believing and evangelizing

---

[1] *Familiaris Consortio*, 70.
[2] Ibid., 21.
[3] Ibid., 49.

community, a community in dialogue with God, and a community at the service of humanity.[4]

A family perspective incorporates a vision of family life that empowers families to realize their identity, mission, and tasks.

Leadership Implications

To develop a family perspective in policies, programs, ministries, and services that takes into account a Christian vision of family life, Church leaders need to:

- Promote families' visions of their own unique mission, sanctity, gifts, and strengths for the service of their own families, the Church, and society.
- Promote the four tasks of the family without over-emphasizing one at the expense of the others, as well as the interconnection of all four tasks.
- Reflect on the tasks of the Christian family, discover concrete activities that families themselves can undertake to accomplish their tasks, and discover some creative ways their own policies, programs, ministries, and services can promote these activities without overburdening families.
- Reflect on and articulate the interconnection between the mission and tasks of the parish community and the "church of the home."

The Second Element: The Family as a Developing System

The family is not a collection of individuals, but a living and developing system whose members are essentially interconnected (see Chapter Five for a fuller explication).

A family perspective assumes that an individual lives connected to others by relationships, not in isolation. Among the most important of these relationships are familial ones. They follow set rules that establish roles and patterns of interaction so that the family can function. These roles and patterns create a positive sense of family identity and promote satisfying and fulfilling relationships among family members. They also facilitate family unity and individual development and contribute to the family's ability to deal effectively with stress. These roles and patterns of interaction are rooted in one's family of origin.

Different kinds of change are also a part of every family's life. Any change in the family, individual, or community affects these roles and patterns, which in turn affects the stability of the family and of each member. Likewise, as families normally grow and develop, as well as encounter events such as death, unemployment, and sickness, they face predictable and unavoidable periods of transition; thus, all fam-

ilies face similar tasks and challenges. The ways in which a family responds to these challenges influence the degree of success it will experience in subsequent ones.

Leadership Implications

To develop a family perspective in policies, programs, ministries, and services that takes into account the family as a developing system, leaders need to:

- Understand they have their own preconceived notions about what a healthy family is. These notions often grow out of their own family experiences. Reflection on their family experiences and on how these affect their vision of family life is essential.
- Become aware of the dynamic interconnection of family members and the power and influence that each member has on other members.
- Be aware of the strengths that exist in each family, so that leaders can help families deepen their strengths.
- Be aware of how families concretely deal with their interpersonal dynamics in order to understand how to support or challenge families who participate in their programs and ministries.
- Appreciate the influence of the family of origin on the individual's way of relating in order to help individuals deal with issues of relationships.
- Be sensitive to the dynamics of the individual's family life cycle stage so that as leaders they can more effectively deal with the individual's and the family's needs.

  For example, in a parish baptismal program, the preparation of a family for the baptism of a first child (the beginning family) is different from the preparation needed by a family whose fourth child is to be baptized (the school-age family).

  Also, couples who were active in parish activities during the years of their children's education commonly relate to their parish in a new way once their children are raised. They face new realities and challenges in their marriage. They also face the issues of aging and retirement. Consequently, their religious and spiritual needs will be different.

- Be aware of the issues, responsibilities, and dynamics multigenerational families face.
- Be able to assess whether the participating individual's family is open or closed to change, since the family can promote or sabotage the efforts of ministry.
- Be aware of the process of change in the family as they work with individuals. By helping an individual change, leaders may be introducing more stress into the person's family.

The Third Element: Family Diversity

Diversity in structure, economic status, special needs, and ethnic and religious heritages and the influence of so-

---

[4] Ibid., 21.

cietal trends affect the roles and activities of families today (see Chapter Six for a fuller explication).

Families are not all alike. Today, they are characterized by diverse structures, needs, economic status, and cultural, ethnic, and religious heritages, and in how they are affected by social change. The result is that families in our nation differ greatly in their values, perceptions, styles, customs, rituals, social norms, shared meanings, life styles, and ways of perceiving the world. Because of these differences, families establish their own roles, responsibilities, and patterns of interaction.

A family perspective names and celebrates the uniqueness in each family. It ensures that policies, programs, ministries, and services take family diversity into account.

Leadership Implications

To develop a family perspective in policies, programs, ministries, and services that takes into account family diversity, leaders need to:

- Keep up to date with family changes and trends in the nation and in their locale, and then examine their policies, programs, ministries, and services in light of this information.
- Be sensitive to the fact that many kinds of families participate in their programs, not only the family that has been called "traditional."
- Be sensitive to the special needs families experience and the pressures and stress these needs create for families. Leaders need to help families identify these pressures and, in partnership, help families deal with them. Particular pastoral care needs to be given to "hurting" families.
- Help families realize that they cannot be fully self-reliant and that it is socially acceptable and responsible to turn to others for help when they experience special needs. Further, leaders need to help families learn to seek help *before* special needs become chronic; preventive ministry needs to be emphasized.
- Be sensitive in planning to the time and energy commitments of families where both parents—or the only parent—are employed.
- Help families deal with the issues raised by social trends such as mobility, the philosophy of individualism and self-fulfillment, the employment of both parents or the only parent, the aging of America, divorce, sexual permissiveness, the women's movement, and changing sex roles.
- Help couples who are in pain and considering divorce to assess realistically their remaining strengths in their marriage and help them find constructive ways of staying together.
- Help couples who have divorced to continue to work together when necessary in order to avoid behavior that is destructive of parent-child and other family relationships. Leaders need to address such

issues as child support, co-parenting, and grandparents' rights.
- Help families who are moving out of the community to leave successfully, and to help families who are moving into the community to adjust successfully. This is especially true for migrant and refugee families.
- Be sensitive to the economic pressures families experience today, particularly the economic distress of unemployed, unemployable, and underemployed persons, as well as the economic stresses that more economically secure families experience.
- Be sensitive to their employees' family situations. Leaders need to develop personnel policies, benefits packages, and job descriptions that support the family life of their employees.
- Be aware of the influences that shape persons' and families' values and behavior. Leaders can develop countercultural experiences that challenge negative and destructive values (e.g., exaggerated competitiveness, individualism, and consumerism).
- Address their policies, programs, ministries, and services to families of different cultural, ethnic, and religious heritages and build their programs on the strengths of these traditions.

The Fourth Element: The Partnership between Families and Social Institutions

Partnerships need to be formed between families and the institutions that share family responsibilities (see Chapter Six for a fuller explication).

Historically, families and kinship groups have taken responsibility for their own basic needs and functions. In the last century, however, many family responsibilities have been shared, transferred, or assumed by public and private institutions. As a result, families and their members spend a great deal of their time, energy, and resources coping with the institutions that now share their responsibilities and coordinating the many services they receive. The policies and programs of many institutions—for example, the government, employment, and service institutions—tend to complicate and fragment family life. A family perspective establishes a working relationship, a partnership between families and those institutions that participate in family responsibilities.

Leadership Implications

To develop a family perspective in policies, programs, ministries, and services that takes into account the partnership between families and social institutions, leaders need to:

- Be sensitive to the fact that even though families and institutions share basic responsibilities, families still retain primary responsibility. Although families may need support and institutional services, these are not the primary responsibility of institutions. Rather, the task of institutions is to support and supplement families in fulfilling their own responsibilities.

- Be aware that families today must seek out a variety of services, from multiple sources, to help them carry out their basic responsibilities. Furthermore, families no longer autonomously set their own standards for these responsibilities; more and more, these standards are defined by professionals, specialists, and social institutions. Families often face great complexity in negotiating multiple services from multiple institutions.
- Understand that *all* programs affect families, even programs aimed at individuals. All social institutions, including the Church, make a direct or indirect impact on the unity, well-being, health, and stability of families. There is a tendency to replace family responsibilities, in part or in their entirety, by social institutions or to marginalize families' participation in the various programs and services provided by these institutions because these services are designed primarily for individuals.
- Help families manage their coordinating and mediating responsibility, rather than complicate it. For example, parish leaders often tell family members that their participation in parish programs is imperative. Therefore, families need to be active participants in determining parish priorities. They also have a responsibility to determine their participation in some parish programs based on a realistic assessment of their energy, family time, and resources.
- Target family and social programs at the mediating structures closest and most accessible to those families, in accordance with the principle of subsidiarity.
- Consider how frequently family members are drawn out of their homes and away from time spent in common. Programs need to build on family presence in the home rather than take family members out of the home even more. Ritual and prayer need to be rooted fundamentally in the home. For example, the *Book of Household Blessings and Prayers*, to be published by the USCC Office of Publishing and Promotion Services in 1988, is a resource that situates family blessing, prayer, and ritual more effectively in the home.
- Promote like-to-like ministry of married couples, family groups, and associations who assist and support families to carry out their responsibilities and to grow in intimacy.

CHAPTER THREE IMPLEMENTING A FAMILY PERSPECTIVE

Once Church and social leaders recognize the elements of a family perspective—(1) a vision of family life; (2) the family as a developing system; (3) family diversity; (4) the partnership between families and social institutions—they are ready to implement a family perspective more systematically. Although there are many ways to accomplish this, the committee offers the following *planned approach* to help leaders, at every level, to ensure that a family perspective lies at the heart of their policies, programs, ministries, and services. This approach needs to include:

1. *Study of the elements* of a family perspective as outlined in this manual.
2. *Reflection on the leadership implications and family impact questions* contained in this manual.
3. *Realistic planning* that incorporates any insights or recommendations from leaders' study and reflection.

Each organization, movement, diocese, and parish within the Church or society needs to decide for itself the most useful and practical way to implement a family perspective. This decision will depend on its own resources and circumstances. However, the committee encourages organizations and movements to consider the following practical ways to accomplish this objective: (1) undertake a family impact study; (2) appoint an advocate for family concerns; (3) convene a family forum; and (4) incorporate family studies into leaders' curriculum of formation, training, and continuing education.

Family Impact Study

"A family impact study is a process of critically and systematically assessing the past, present, or probable future effects of a policy, program, ministry, or service (as well as procedures and training programs) on family members, family relationships, and family responsibilities."[1] An organization can engage in such a study on two levels. On the first level, family impact questions, such as those contained in this manual, need to be reframed so as to be relevant to the particular policy, program, ministry, or service that is under study. Then the policy or program can be reviewed in light of these questions. For example, a youth minister could review the organization's youth policy, program, or service with these or other family impact questions:

- How does it address the adolescent's needs, the needs of the adolescent in relation to his or her family, and the needs of the entire family?
- How does it make itself aware of and eliminate any stereotypes or negative attitudes concerning particular family situations (for example, single-parent households, divorced families, blended families, ethnic families, ecumenical or interfaith families, and dual career families)?
- How does it help the teenagers and their families deal with the change promoted by the program, as well as to mediate the tensions inherent in parent-teen relationships?
- How does it involve the parents of the teens in its planning, implementation, and evaluation?

Other family impact questions are at the end of Chapters Four through Seven.

On the second level, leaders enter into a more detailed and formal family impact study,[2] a seven-step process that includes: (1) forming a working group to conduct the study; (2) developing a study design and action plan; (3) developing key family impact questions; (4) gathering and reviewing the data; (5) developing and reviewing the findings; (6) developing the recommendations; and (7) implementing the results of the study.

Within the parish community, it is recommended family impact studies be undertaken by the parish staff, council, and committees. On a diocesan level, these studies need to be done by the diocesan departments and secretariats. Of special importance are the ministries of health care, education, the tribunal, catechesis, and social and pastoral services. On a national level, all major organizations and movements need to undertake these family impact studies, especially in the areas of policy, training, and resource development. Examples of efforts to incorporate a

---

[1] T. Ooms, *A General Educational Guide to Family Impact Studies* (Washington, D.C.: The National Center for Family Studies at The Catholic University of America, 1985).

[2] Ibid.

family perspective into the policy of national organizations are the bishops' pastoral letter *Economic Justice for All*[3] and the collaborative document, *The Challenge of Adolescent Catechesis: Maturing in Faith.*[4]

The Family Advocate and the Family Life Minister

The committee recommends the appointment of a family advocate within each of the departments of organizations, dioceses, and parishes. A family advocate is an individual who is responsible for the family dimension of that particular department. For example, a parish or a diocese may appoint a family advocate within its religious education program. A family advocate's responsibility will usually be only a part of the person's fuller job description within the department. However, the individual must be allotted realistic time to accomplish the family-centered aspect of the department's ministry. To influence effectively future or present policies, programs, ministries, or services, the family advocate must have access to the department's decision-making process.

Family advocates have two major responsibilities. The first is to articulate the realities families face today to the department's leadership and thus to facilitate the adjustments that may need to take place within the department's policies, programs, ministries, and services. The second is to develop the underlying family component inherent in the department's ministry. For example, the following is a partial list of departments' family components in a diocese or parish:

1. Disability: the families of disabled persons.
2. Ecumenical: interfaith and ecumenical families.
3. Education: family life education.
4. Health: family health care.
5. Liturgy: family ritual, prayer, and celebration.
6. Multicultural: for example, Hispanic, black, Asian families.
7. Religious Education: family catechesis.
8. Social Development: family social policy, neighborhood and community environment conducive to healthy family life.
9. Social Services: marriage and family counseling, family supports and services.
10. Young Adult Ministry: engaged and young married, young adults and their relationships with their families of origin.
11. Youth Ministry: parent, sibling, and teen relations.

---

[3] National Conference of Catholic Bishops, *Economic Justice for All: Pastoral Letter on Catholic Social Teaching and the U.S. Economy* (Washington, D.C.: USCC Office of Publishing and Promotion Services, 1986).

[4] National Federation for Catholic Youth Ministry, National Catholic Educational Association, and National Conference of Diocesan Directors of Religious Education, *The Challenge of Adolescent Catechesis: Maturing in Faith,* 1986.

A family advocate needs to be trained in or exposed to family studies. These studies include family systems; the history and sciences that explicate family relations; family services; pastoral ministries; and a theology of marriage and family life that is rooted in Catholic tradition. Often, a department will not have a person trained in these areas of family studies. The need remains to have a trained person, but this training may have to take place over a longer period of time through continuing education or enrollment in a formal program. Therefore, it is important to be realistic in what the department is able to accomplish as it tries to incorporate a family perspective.

Appointing family advocates does not eliminate the need for the designated family life minister and family life office within an organization, diocese, or parish. On the contrary, family advocates need a special relationship with the family life minister. To understand the purpose of this relationship, it is important to note the role of the family life minister.

The major responsibility of the family life minister and the family life office within the organization, diocese, or parish is to promote total ministry to, with, by, and for families (including worship, catechesis, political advocacy, education, health care, welfare, and enrichment). The family minster also needs to:

- Implement the marriage and family policies and programs of the universal Church and the bishops of the United States: for example, the *Plan of Pastoral Action for Family Ministry; Familiaris Consortio; The Charter of the Rights of the Family;* and *A Family Perspective in Church and Society.*
- Develop and promote a Christian vision of family life in a way that is meaningful and enabling to the constituent families of the organization, diocese, or parish.
- Coordinate organization-, diocesan-, or parish-wide services to families in order to eliminate duplication, waste of families' time, energy, and money, and the fragmentation of families' members. The family life minister and the family advocates can form and convene a family life committee to coordinate the family efforts throughout the entire organization, diocese, or parish. This will also provide a vehicle for collaborative undertakings on behalf of families.
- Identify gaps in family services and assess the organization's, diocese's, or parish's ability to fill them.
- Disseminate current information and research data about family life, including what is being learned by regularly and systematically listening to families themselves as required by the *Plan of Pastoral Action for Family Ministry.* This information also includes developments in family ministries taking place throughout the organization.
- Assist the organization's departments as they develop their family component, for example, co-sponsoring a family social policy committee with the office of social development or consulting with a family life education committee sponsored by the office of education.

- Participate in professional associations and continuing education opportunities, in order to promote the development of family ministry and to enhance the professional competence needed for family ministry.
- Serve as a liaison to other national and local religious and secular organizations that relate to family life. This will provide a broader base for consultation, sharing, enrichment, networking, and advocacy on behalf of families.
- Assume the role of an advocate when a department does not have one. The family minister can assist the department, as well as urge that a member of the staff be promoted to the role of family advocate.

The family life minister brings a particular vision to his or her ministry: namely, that families are called to be ministers to themselves and to other families. This vision was promoted in the *Plan of Pastoral Action for Family Ministry* and *Familiaris Consortio* and is based on the principle that individuals with similar life experiences can support and minister to each other; for example, parents who have lost a child, newly married couples, the divorced. To implement like-to-like ministry, the family life minister needs to:

- Initiate and oversee the formation of groups of people with similar experiences: recruit, train, supervise, and support group leaders; determine when the groups are no longer necessary and facilitate a positive closure of the group.
- Help these groups and other grass-roots family organizations to form associations or small faith communities. The family life minister ecourages families themselves to become more active in supporting, asserting, and protecting their rights.[5] In this effort, the skills of community organization can prove especially useful. The family life minister encourages families and associations to organize politically so that they will have a greater voice within the institutions and services that share their responsibilities. This will also fulfill families' basic task of participating in the development of society. *The Charter of the Rights of the Family* explicates the rights that need to be protected by both society and the family.[6]

Family Forum

To promote the incorporation of a family perspective, an organization, diocese, parish, or movement can convene a family forum. A family forum provides an opportunity for families who are connected with the organization to come together to share their stories. It also provides an opportunity for families to share how particular policies, programs, ministries, or services of the organization affect them. This forum can be the basis for ongoing listening to families as well as a vehicle to promote a renewed partnership between the organization and the families it serves.

To help assure the relevancy and sensitivity of the family forum to the concerns of families, the organization could form a steering committee. It could be comprised of persons from different kinds of families within the organization's constituency to work with the designated family minister or advocate in establishing the location, frequency, format, and agenda for the family forum. In dioceses and parishes, the family forum could elect one of its members to serve on the parish and pastoral councils.

Family Studies

Finally, to ensure that a family perspective is built into organizations, dioceses, parishes, and movements for the future, it is important to integrate family studies into leaders' curricula of formation, training, and continuing education. Such studies will prepare leaders to recognize and address the needs of families. By family studies is meant a basic understanding of family systems; the history and sciences that explicate family relations; family services; pastoral ministries; and a theological understanding of marriage and family life as rooted in the tradition of the Catholic Church. Incorporating family studies into training curricula does not mean adding more courses to an already full program. However, it does require adjusting existing courses so they incorporate a family dimension:

- *Canon Law:* serious attention to c. 1063 and its implication for parish ministry. This canon states:

  > Pastors of souls are obliged to see to it that their own ecclesial community furnishes the Christian faithful assistance so that the matrimonial state is maintained in a Christian spirit and makes progress toward perfection. This assistance is especially to be furnished through:
  > 1° preaching, catechesis adapted to minors, youths and adults, and even the use of the media of social communications so that through these means the Christian faithful may be instructed concerning the meaning of Christian marriage and the duty of Christian spouses and parents;
  > 2° personal preparation for entering marriage so that through such preparation the parties may be predisposed toward the holiness and duties of their new state;
  > 3° a fruitful liturgical celebration of marriage clarifying that the spouses signify and share in that mystery of unity and of fruitful love that exists between Christ and the Church;
  > 4° assistance furnished to those already married so that, while faithfully maintaining and protecting the conjugal convenant, they may day by day come to lead holier and fuller lives in their families.[7]

[5] *Familiaris Consortio*, 44.

[6] Vatican, *Charter of the Rights of the Family* (Washington, D.C.: USCC Office of Publishing and Promotion Services, 1983).

[7] Canon Law Society of America, *Code of Canon Law, Latin-English Edition* (Washington: D.C.: Canon Law Society of America, 1983), c. 1063.

- *Catechesis:* the role of parents as ministers and primary educators, and the development of family catechesis.
- *Church History:* the history of the church of the home and how Christian families have changed and developed over the centuries.
- *Ecclesiology:* the sacredness of family life and its inherent ecclesial dimension and ministry.
- *Ecumenism:* the opportunities and stresses inherent in ecumenical and interfaith marriages, pastoral support for ecumenical and interfaith families, and a study of the marriage and family traditions of other communions.
- *Liturgy:* the ritual and symbolic activity of the household, family prayer and worship, and the connection between parish communal worship and the worship of the church of the home.
- *Pastoral Counseling:* the theory and practice of marriage and family counseling.
- *Pastoral Field Placements:* preparation of ministers who can initiate, supervise, and train leaders to facilitate like-to-like family ministry.
- *Pastoral Theology:* the family as a subject of ministry, as well as the object of parish ministry, the empowerment of families regarding their four tasks identified in *Familiaris Consortio.*
- *Psychology and Human Development:* family systems theory, the family life cycle, and family diversity.
- *Sacraments, and especially the Sacrament of Marriage:* the inherent sacredness of marriage and family life, the family as the church of the home with its own unique identity, mission, and tasks.
- *Spirituality:* family spirituality, rooted in the sacredness of the ordinary.

Level Two Development of the Elements of a Family Perspective

Level Two presents a deeper understanding of the four elements of a family perspective (Chapters Four through Seven).

- The *Family Impact Questions* found at the end of each of these chapters will assist readers as they work to incorporate a family perspective in their policies, programs, ministries, and services.

CHAPTER FOUR
THE FIRST ELEMENT: A CHRISTIAN VISION OF FAMILY LIFE

A Christian vision of family life is the first essential element of a family perspective for the Christian community. It is a vision that the Church offers in dialogue with persons and institutions that hold other visions.

Context of Faith

Social scientists view the family as it is. That is, they describe its structure, its origin, its problems, and its tasks. Their view is descriptive. Theologians proceed differently. Their view is normative. They say how the family ought to be and propose a Christian vision of family life. Their starting point is not the charts and tables of the sociologist, but a vision of human growth through God's grace. This vision bears examining.

The Book of Genesis tells us that God created human beings in the divine image: "Male and Female God created them," with the blessing to be fruitful, multiply, and fill the earth. By this act, God made family life sacred. Christians believe that human beings were made by God for God. However, they also believe that, by the first sin, human beings turned from God into themselves. This selfish action inflicted on human nature a wound whose healing (conversion or reconciliation with God through Christ) has become the heart of the Christian life.

Yet, even though the human race had lost its friendship with God through the first or original sin, God, as the words of Eucharistic Prayer IV say, ". . . did not abandon [us] to the power of death," but gave us the means "to seek and find [God]. Again and again [God] offered a covenant," a covenant which reached its fulfillment in the coming of the savior, Jesus Christ. This new covenant, established in the death and resurrection of the savior, is the model for marriage and family life.

This marital covenant, founded on the life of Christ, brought about by free human choice, and ratified by divine assistance, is realized in the sacrament of marriage and family life:

> Christ himself entrusts to this domestic church, the family, a specific and original role within the Church that is his body. The family's task is "to build up the kingdom of God in history through the everyday realities that concern and distinguish its state of life" (*Familiaris Consortio*, 50). In developing this theme, Pope John Paul II, drawing on the teaching of Vatican II and Pope Paul VI, stresses that the specific conjugal love of the spouses—the love meant to be expressed in their lives and extended through their family and children to the community in which they live—is what "constitutes the nucleus of the saving mission of the Christian family in the Church and for the Church" (ibid.). Thus, to understand the specific and original role within the Church of the Christian family, it is necessary to reflect on the specific nature of conjugal and spousal love. The characteristics of this love, beautifully set forth in *The Church in the Modern World*, *Humanae Vitae*, and the writings of Pope John Paul II, may be summed up by saying that spousal or marital or conjugal love is a specific form of human friendship love that is unique because it is sacramental and redemptive, exclusive, and fruitful or procreative.[1]

In recent years, the Church has reemphasized both the nobility and importance of marriage in the life of the Church and also the central role of the spouses in creating and maintaining the marriage relationship. The Second Vatican Council spoke of "the intimate partnership of married life and love . . . rooted in the conjugal covenant of irrevocable personal consent."[2] Pope John Paul II has described marriage as "the convenant of conjugal love freely and consciously chosen, whereby men and women accept the intimate community of life and love willed by God himself."[3]

In addition to considering the divine plan for the spouses themselves, the Church has also been concerned with the full social dimension of marriage and family life. *The Charter of the Rights of the Family* (hereafter referred to as the *Charter*)—produced by the Holy See at the request of the 1980 Synod of Bishops, which discussed the family—presents the rights of the family both as a vision of the way things should be and as a norm for legislation and social policy. The *Charter* begins by stating that "the rights of the person, even though they are expressed as rights of the individual, have a fundamental social dimension which finds an

---

[1] W. May, "Role of the Christian Family, Articles 49-58" in *Pope John Paul II and the Family* (Chicago: Franciscan Herald Press, 1981), 171-172.

[2] Second Vatican Council, *Gaudium et Spes* ("Pastoral Constitution on the Church in the Modern World") in *The Documents of Vatican II*, W. M. Abbott, SJ, ed. (Piscataway, N.J.: New Century Publishers, Inc., 1966), 48.

[3] *Familiaris Consortio*, 11.

innate and vital expression in the family. . . ." The family "exists prior to the state or any other community, and possesses rights which are inalienable. . . ."[4]

The social dimension of the family cannot be limited to civil society. In the Church, this social dimension is manifested by seeing the family as an authentic church community, a "domestic church," and therefore a community that seeks to bring about the Kingdom of God in the world. This church of the home provides, prepares, nourishes, and sustains the members of both the Church and civil society.

Definition of Family

Defining the family proves to be a more difficult task than it appears. As the 1980 White House Conference on Families demonstrated, defining the family is not only sociologically difficult but politically charged as well. It is sociologically difficult because the criteria customarily used to define family membership are undergoing change.

The Church itself is no stranger to changes in family definition. Until recently, the Church, like much of Western society, drew on the principle of Roman law that defined family membership by reference to the family head as the family's cohesive force. Those who were under the authority of the family head were members of that family, and the power or authority of the head was a major social value.

However, the Church has changed this authority-focused view. As noted, the Second Vatican Council spoke of marriage as an intimate union of life and love. The revised *Code of Canon Law* describes marriage, and thus the family, as a partnership of equality, and the significance of this equality should not be missed. Because of the normative role of sacramental marriage in defining family roles, this view of marriage proves most useful in providing a Christian foundation for a consideration of family membership. This view of marriage as a partnership of equality is also reflected in *Familiaris Consortio*. In this statement, Pope John Paul II defines the family, in which marriage is its foundation, as that intimate community of life and love. The family's first task is always to form a community of persons in mutual self-giving.

The definition of family life used in this manual, below, is intended to reflect current church legislation and to be consistent with Christian beliefs, and thus to reflect faithfully what is of divine origin for family life. To do all this, the definition must be exclusive enough to maintain its real meaning. The term "family" (or "family life") does not include the more symbolic uses of the word *family* that are drawn by analogy from family life, such as the need all persons have for intimacy and community. It excludes metaphors, such as the parish as a family. It must also be broad enough

to include the variety of families and family situations in our society.

Drawing on *Familiaris Consortio* and Catholic tradition, this manual defines the family as an intimate community of persons bound together by blood, marriage, or adoption, for the whole of life. In our Catholic tradition, the family proceeds from marriage—an intimate, exclusive, permanent, and faithful partnership of husband and wife. This definition is intentionally normative and recognizes that the Church's normative approach is not shared by all.

This definition does not limit the family to two generations, parent and child, living in the same household. It proposes a broader view:

- It includes other relatives as well as ancestors and crosses the family life cycle. In fact, the definition is broad enough to recognize that family ties bind tightly, even when members live in different households.
- It recognizes that many persons are involved simultaneously in several families, a fact that can be complicating as well as supporting, since each family can require support as well as provide it.
- It also includes single persons since they too have families and are involved in the lives and needs of their family members. While many single persons live in their own households at a distance from family members, this manual is also addressed to them and their relationship with their family of origin, which continues to have a powerful effect on how they relate to themselves, to God, and to others.
- It also recognizes that there are other covenantal relationships in the family besides marriage, for example, the relationship between parents and children, siblings, grandparents, and family dependents. In many cases, these relationships can last longer than the marriage relationship itself, especially in the event of the death of a spouse.
- Finally, the definition acknowledges the special relationships established in families that are created by adoption, which mirrors the image used by St. Paul (e.g., Rom 8:23; Gal 4:5). These families respond to the need in our society to bring into families those people who have none or whose birth families cannot meet their needs.

Prophetic Role of the Christian Family

The committee recognizes that this definition of the family contains views that are countercultural. They represent an important departure from definitions of the family based on notions of social production and authority. The view that the family exists to serve the needs of the state, while foreign to the American situation, is still common enough elsewhere in the world to merit attention and rejection. The view that the

---

[4] *Charter of the Rights of the Family*, Preamble.

family is to be principally a school in willing obedience to its head and all authority, or the view that the family is to provide another generation of good stewards for the family's possessions—views more prevalent in our society—both contrast with the mission described by Pope John Paul II. Likewise, the view that the family is a temporary community of individual self-interest is also wholly foreign to Christian understanding. Pope John Paul II's definition is adaptable to diverse arrangements of family structures and responsibilities, providing that "the family be a community of life and love, that guards, communicates, and reveals that love."[5]

Pope John Paul II has enlarged upon the four general family tasks given by the 1980 Synod on the Family,[6] developing a notion of the family's mission in the world. Because of the Christian challenge so evident in these tasks, an idealism that places the family in the forefront of social renewal, they are included here under the heading of the family's prophetic role.

Task 1: The family is an intimate community of persons.

This community is manifested in mutual self-giving by the members of the family throughout its life together. It calls for a faithful and permanent love among all family members, rooted in the complementarity and equality of husband and wife. It challenges an exaggerated individualism by calling all members to mutual self-giving in order to contribute to the life and vitality of the family and to individual members. This community also calls for the respect of each family member's uniqueness and dignity. Special attention must be given to the rights and dignity of every member, especially children, the sick, the disabled, and other dependents. It is essential that the elderly be respected and provided loving care as well as given the opportunity to contribute to the family's and society's well-being.

Task 2: The family serves life in its transmission, both physically by bringing children into the world, and spiritually by handing on values and traditions as well as developing the potential of each member at every age.

Husbands and wives truly love each other when they are responsible before God and carry out God's plan for human life and love. The love between husband and wife must be "fully human, total, exclusive, faithful and open to life."[7] Further, responsible parenthood involves not only bringing children into the world but also taking part personally and responsibly in their upbringing and education. According to Vatican II, the role of parents in education has such importance that it is almost impossible to provide an adequate substitute. It is therefore the duty of parents to create a family atmosphere inspired by love and devotion to God and their fellow persons, which will promote an integrated, personal and social education of the child. "Hence, parents must be acknowledged as the first and foremost educators of their children."[8] However, the formational task is not limited solely to parenting. It is the responsibility of all members of the family to promote the development and potential of each member at every age.

Task 3: The family participates in the development of society by becoming a community of social training, hospitality, and political involvement and activity.

Because the family is the first and principal school of training in social virtues, it is the most effective means for humanizing and personalizing society. How family members learn to relate to each other with respect, love, caring, fidelity, honesty, and commitment becomes their way of relating to others in the world.[9]

When the family is a community of hospitality, it responds generously to the hungry and the abandoned. A growing privatization and individualization within American society has led to a regrettable willingness within families to close their doors to needy relatives and to consider all other needy the responsibility of the state.[10] The Christian family sees the care of the needy as a normal part of its vocation. As the bishops' pastoral letter *Economic Justice for All* states: "At times we will be called as individuals, as families, as parishes, as Church, to identify more closely with the poor in their struggle for participation and to close the gap of understanding between them and the affluent."[11]

Since the family is a community of political involvement, it is required to enter into the life of society in a creative and active way:

Families should be the first to take steps to see that laws and institutions of the state not only do not offend, but support and positively defend the rights and duties of the family. Along these lines families should grow in awareness of being "protagonists" of what is known as "family politics" and assume responsibility for transforming society; otherwise families will be the first victims of the evils that they have done no more than note with indifference.[12]

---

[5] *Familiaris Consortio*, 17.

[6] 1980 Synod of Bishops, *The Role of the Christian Family in the Modern World*, a Study Guide (Washington, D.C.: USCC Office of Publishing and Promotion Services, 1980).

[7] Paul VI, *On the Regulation of Birth* (Washington, D.C.: USCC Office of Publishing and Promotion Services, 1968), 9.

[8] Second Vatican Council, *Gravissimum Educationis* ("Declaration on Christian Education") in *Documents of Vatican II*, 3.

[9] M. L. King, Jr., "Address" at Abbot House, Westchester County, New York (October 1965) in *Family and Nation* (New York: Harcourt Brace Jovanovich, 1986).

[10] Haraven, *The Diversity and Strength of American Families*, 29.

[11] *Economic Justice for All*, 335.

[12] *Familiaris Consortio*, 44.

Task 4: The family shares in the life and mission of the Church by becoming a believing and evangelizing community, a community in dialogue with God, and a community at the service of humanity.

By sharing in the life and mission of the Church, the family is the church of the home. In a homily in Perth, Australia, Pope John Paul II made the following statement:

The family is the domestic church. The meaning of this traditional Christian idea is that the home is the Church in miniature. The Church is the sacrament of God's love. She is a communion of faith and love. She is a mother and teacher. She is at the service of the whole human family as it goes forward towards its ultimate destiny. In the same way the family is a community of life and love. It educates and leads its members to their full human maturity and it serves the good of all along the road of life. In its own way it is a living image and historical representation of the mystery of the Church. The future of the world and of the Church pass way of the family.[13]

This papal teaching renews a major theme in Catholic theology. It calls for reform in any church or parish program that does not recognize the authenticity of the family as the church of the home. This teaching contains two principles that can serve as guidelines both to restore the proper role of the family in the Church and to develop the partnership between the Church and families: (1) family life is sacred and family activities are holy; (2) the Christian family, as the church of the home, has a unique ministry.

The principle of family life as sacred and family activities as holy speaks to the meaning of family spirituality:

The ordinary experiences and activities of family living can and do reveal the sacred. Look at any point within the broad range of our families. Most of the significant human events occur there. Birth and death, marriage and childhood, sickness and unemployment—these are but a few of the ordinary events of life, and all form a family spirituality. Each event has a potential to open up and reveal the sacred. Each presents an opportunity to recognize and celebrate the Love at the heart of family life.

The family meal is an example of the sacred in the ordinary, and an opportunity to know one another in the breaking of the bread—to have intimacy with the Lord through intimacy with one another. In the sharing of ordinary food and conversation the sacred is likely to emerge, from one day to the next. . . .

Ordinary daily events have a deep natural holiness waiting to be unlocked, as does taking time to reflect on the day that is just beginning or just drawing to a close. Times of forgiveness and reconciliation are fertile ground for recognizing the presence of the Healer. Small, sometimes momentary ways to evoke the sacred in these and many other ordinary family events can be created by a family that tries to be sensitive to the inherent holiness of their life together.[14]

The principle of the Christian family as the church of the home, a church that has its own unique ministry, has been strongly supported by papal documents, theological insights, and a renewed understanding of Scripture and tradition. As already seen, the Church is recovering and renewing the idea of the domestic church as an authentic ecclesial community.[15] The family is not merely like the Church, but is truly Church. Karl Rahner wrote: "The Church becomes present in marriage: marriage is really the smallest community of the redeemed and the sanctified . . . hence, it is truly the smallest individual church."[16]

The Fathers of Vatican II revived the concept of the family as the domestic Church,[17] a concept rooted in Scripture, Judaism, and the traditions of the early Church. The earliest Christians were converts from Judaism, and the center of Jewish religious life (particularly after the destruction of the temple A.D. 70) was the home, not the synagogue. So it makes sense that the early Jewish Christians would hold family life in the highest esteem.

The Acts of the Apostles and the letters of St. Paul reflect positive attitudes toward family life that must have been so common as to have simply been taken for granted. "The household," write scripture scholars Elisabeth and Louis Tetlow, "was the basic unit of the Christian community in the first century. It was the household, the family, that heard and accepted, lived and taught, the Gospel of Jesus."

As early as the late fourth century, St. John Chrysostom named the family *ecclesia*, and consistent with this ancient teaching, in the late nineteenth century, Pope Leo XIII called the family "the first form of the church on earth.[18]

Just as the institutional Church calls all levels of society to follow the principle of subsidiarity, the Church also needs to follow this principle of subsidiarity in its relationship to the family. Thus, the diocesan church cannot and should not do what the parish church can rightly do better. Nor should the diocesan or parish church do for the church of the home what it can rightly do for itself and the Church.[19]

The ministry of the family as the church of the home is rooted in its identity, mission, tasks, and responsibilities. As Pope John Paul II tells us: "Among the fundamental tasks of the Christian family is its eccle-

[13] John Paul II, "Homily" delivered in Perth, Australia, November 30, 1986.

[14] M. Finley and K. Finley, "The Sacredness of the Ordinary," *Family Spirituality: The Sacred in the Ordinary* (National Association of Catholic Diocesan Family Life Ministers, 1984), 70-71.

[15] *Familiaris Consortio*, 15.

[16] K. Rahner, *Foundations of Christian Faith*, 421.

[17] *Gaudium et Spes*, 11, 48.

[18] M. Finley, "Family Orphaned by the Church" in *National Catholic Reporter* (Kansas City, Mo. [February 28, 1986]): 11-12.

[19] M. Iannone, "The Dearest Freshness: Images of Family Life from a Faith Perspective" in *Families and Television: A Book of Readings*, F. Brigham, Jr., and S. Preister, eds. (Washington, D.C.: The National Center for Family Studies at The Catholic University of America, 1987).

sial task: the family is placed at the service of building up the kingdom of God in history by participating in the life and mission of the Church."[20]

In this call to participate in the Church's life, ministry is recognized as an integral part of Christian family life. According to *Familiaris Consortio*, ministry is an inherent call given to all Christian families, especially given to parents in their irreplaceable and primary formation of their children.[21] Families minister first to their own members, but that priority is not strict or exclusive. Families need to keep in mind that the family-by-adoption, as the Holy Family exemplifies and St. Paul explains at length, is the prime model in Christian life. Consequently, the Christian family is called to be a model of generosity and charity to those in need, especially to those in need of what the family is, a community of love, and of what the family, in fact, has—love.

The family is also called to develop in the hearts of its members an openness and willingness to serve the Church in the particular roles of the ordained and the consecrated life. Vocations to the priesthood, diaconate, and consecrated life are to be fostered through family prayer and encouragement.

This insight about the family as the church of the home is not a surprising one. The Church is essentially a community of believing persons, joined in relationship in fulfillment of the Lord's command to love one another. As the basic community of believers, bound in love to one another, the family is the arena in which the drama of redemption is played out. The dying and rising with Christ is most clearly manifested. Here, the cycle of sin, hurt, reconciliation, and healing is lived out over and over again. In family life is found the church of the home: where each day "two or three are gathered" in the Lord's name; where the hungry are fed; where the thristy are given drink; where the sick are comforted. It is in the family that the Lord's injunction to forgive "seventy times seven" is lived out in the daily reconciliation of husband, wife, parent, child, grandparent, brothers, sisters, extended kin.[22]

---

[20] *Familiaris Consortio*, 49.
[21] Ibid., 36, 38-39.
[22] T. Boland, Unpublished Personal Notes (Louisville: Family Life Office, 1986).

The Family as a Community of Redemption

An asceticism resides at the very heart of Christian marriage and family life. This asceticism is not that of the stoic—a discipline undertaken for social utility or personal growth. Rather, this asceticism, whose purpose comes from God, is open only to the eyes of faith. This asceticism is rooted in the life commitments made by men and women, commitments that need not have been made or that could have been made differently, that can and must be kept. They are kept as the individual's own and as the couple's way to participate in the redeeming work of Christ. By freely keeping these commitments in Christ and thru Christ, the wound of original sin is healed.

Family Impact Questions

To incorporate a family perspective that takes into account a Christian vision of family life, leaders need to ask questions such as the following about their specific policy, program, ministry, or service:

- How does it state a vision of family life that is faithful to Christian tradition?
- In what ways does it develop within the family both a greater appreciation of family activities as sacred and also a better understanding of the family's ecclesial mission?
- How does it promote the unique ministry of the family?
- How does it promote the tasks of the family without overburdening families?
- How does it help spouses to remain faithful to the Church's teaching regarding their responsibilities for the transmission of life?
- In what ways does it promote the knowledge and skills that can enable a participating family to become a more effective community of persons?
- How does it promote the development of family prayer, ritual, and celebration?
- In what concrete ways does it promote the organization of families into small faith communities and help them to be more politically active in protecting the rights of all families?
- How does it enable families to be more effective in handing on their values and traditions?

CHAPTER FIVE
THE SECOND ELEMENT:
THE FAMILY AS A
DEVELOPING SYSTEM

The second element of a family perspective is recognizing the family as a system:

A system is anything that constitutes a cluster of highly interrelated parts, each responding to the other while at the same time somehow maintaining itself as a whole even when there is incessant internal change. The three parts of the definition [of a system] are: the parts are in relationship with one another; the whole is greater than the sum of the parts; and, the whole is able to continue and change in response to itself and to its environment.[1]

A systems approach elevates the interaction and cooperation among the members of the whole to a place of prominence and places less emphasis upon the solitary action of the individual. It does not see the whole as merely a collection of individuals, but as a system of relationships, expectations, and responsibilities by which people connect the very heart of who they are to other people.

This is at the very heart of our understanding of family from the beginning. God created male *and* female and in that act(s) was created the mystery that is known as the family. One cannot understand a family or minister to that family until one understands the nature of *"and"* and the dynamics of relationships that *"and"* implies.[2]

Thus, a family is more than the sum of its parts. It is a dynamic and developing system whose members are radically interdependent. Individuals participate in their systems rather than being mere parts. The way one person depends on another, the fact that a person acts independently, the health of a parent, the aging and illness of a family member, a child's maturing and leaving home—all these events in the life of one or another family member have an effect on the lives of all family members. St. Paul, in his letters, captures this understanding:

As a body is one though it has many parts, and all the parts of the body, though many, are one body, so also Christ (1 Cor 12:12).
For as in one body we have many parts, and all the parts do not have the same function, so we, though many, are one body in Christ and individually parts of one another. . . . we have gifts that differ according to the grace given to us . . . (Rom 12:4-6).
. . . God has so constructed the body as to give greater honor to a part that is without it, so that there may be no division in the body, but that the parts may have the same concern for one another. If [one] part suffers, all the parts suffer with it; if one part is honored, all the parts share its joy (1 Cor 12:24-26).

Like all other systems, family systems operate according to rules. These rules are either explicit and recognized by family members, or they are implicit. They determine roles and interactional patterns that individual family members are expected to fulfill. To understand a family as a system requires not only gathering data about characteristics of the individual members but also focusing on how the members interrelate with one another. Further, these relationships constantly evolve and change. Any change in a family, or in a family member, or in a family's environment affects the life and functioning of the family and each of its members. Therefore, the issues that are present in the life of a family must be part of the agenda of those who are working with any member of a family.

For church and social leaders to incorporate the systems element of a family perspective into policies, programs, ministries, and services, they need to understand how each of the following dynamics operates in family systems: (1) family strengths; (2) family health; (3) the family of orgin; (4) the family life cycle; and (5) family change.

Family Strengths

Each family member needs nurturance, autonomy, and intimacy, as well as life-giving ways of obtaining them. This is why families are the source of so much comfort, support, and love, as well the source of so much tension, pain, and anger. All families manifest these qualities at different times because of their ability or inability to respond adequately to the needs of members and to the needs of the family as a whole.

---

[1] D. Guernsey, *A New Design for Family Ministry* (Elgin, Ill.: David Cook Publishers, 1982), 67.
[2] Ibid., 66.

Researchers have identified important characteristics of families that enable them to operate effectively.[3] These characteristics are referred to as family strengths. Family strengths can be defined as those relational patterns, interpersonal skills, attitudes, competencies, values, and individual psychological characteristics that help the family to work. These strengths allow the family to cope with stress, change, and problems in a caring and effective way.

> The family has the ability to handle the daily hassles and events that come along but also are able to handle the more typical stressors that occur across the life cycle. This may include adjusting to the birth of a child, dealing with rebellion of an adolescent, and adapting to the changing roles of a mother as she may move from homemaker to the workplace. It also means being able to deal with nonnormative events such as illnesses or injuries which often have an immense impact on a family system.[4]

Certain characteristics within the family have been identified as strengths.[5] They have been summarized below. They include the ability of the family to:

- appreciate and respect each other;
- spend both quality and quantity of time together;
- develop and use skills in communication, negotiating and resolving problems and differences in a positive and constructive way;
- develop a strong sense of commitment to stay related during times of transition, difficulty, or crisis;
- possess a solid core of moral and spiritual beliefs; and
- rely on other resources such as the social network, which includes family, friends and kin, as well as community resources such as churches and other helping agencies.

The above mentioned family strengths have positive effects on the family. They assist in the development of a positive self-image, promote satisfying and fulfilling interaction among family members, and encourage the development of the potential of the family group and its individual members.

Family Health

Family strengths lead to family health, the second dynamic operative in family systems. Family strengths, and ultimately family health, develop because a family is both cohesive and adaptive.

"Family cohesion is the emotional bonding that family members have with one another and the relative degree of autonomy a person experiences in a [family] system."[6] A family lives in a dynamic balance between being too connected (enmeshed) or too separated (disengaged). When a family is enmeshed, the members are not allowed to possess an individual identity other than that of the family's. Members constantly live out the expectations of the family without any appreciation of themselves as unique persons with their own strengths and weaknesses. When a family is disengaged, the individual has little sense of or appreciation for the family as a whole. The person sees no connection between him or herself and other family members. Family members simply coexist in the same space. Cohesion is worked out concretely by a family around the following issues:[7]

- *Support.* What kind of support is each member expected to give or receive?
- *Closeness.* What kind of self-disclosure is each member expected to give or receive?
- *Decision Making.* How and by whom are decisions made?
- *Commonality.* How much are family members expected to do in common?
- *Unity.* How much are family members expected to be identified with the family?

The following story, told by a young married woman, is an example of how cohesion is worked out in a family.

> When I got married, I tried to reserve a psychological space that was just mine—something that would keep me from being so involved with my husband that I could not separate one from the other. I was afraid that if anything happened to him, I would not be able to cope unless I could keep from sharing everything with him. Over the past five years of my marriage, I've changed my mind, because I began to believe that I was only cheating the two of us out of the best relationship we could have. I realize that David is willing to love me as fully as possible, so I've grown to take the risk to respond as fully as possible. It still frightens me, though.[8]

Cohesion also pertains to how open or closed the family is to other social networks (friends, extended kin, churches, and helping agencies). The same issues of support, closeness, decision making, commonality, and unity are worked out among the family and its members and the various communities to which they belong.

The other base of family health is adaptability. "Adaptability is . . . the ability of a system to change

---

[3] For summary, see E. A. Morgan, *Pioneer Research on Strong, Healthy Families* (Washington, D.C.: The Family Research Council, 1987).

[4] D. H. Olson, *The Diversity and Strength of American Families*, 104.

[5] For summary, see *Pioneer Research on Strong, Healthy Families*; D. Curran, *Traits of the Healthy Family* (Minneapolis: Winston Press, 1983); N. Stinnett, "In Search of Strong Families, *Building Family Strengths: Blueprints for Action* (Lincoln: University of Nebraska Press, 1979), 23-30; N. Stinnett, "Strong Families: A Portrait," *Prevention in Family Services: Approaches to Family Wellness* (Beverly Hills, Calif.: Sage Publications, 1983), 27-38; N. Stinnett, et al., "Relationship Characteristics of Strong Families" in *Family Perspective* 11 (1977): 3-11; N. Stinnett et al., "Strong Families: A National Study," *Family Strengths 3: Roots of Family Well-Being* (Lincoln: University of Nebraska Press, 1981), 33-41.

[6] *A New Design for Family Ministry*, 101.

[7] P. Carnes, *Family Development I: Understanding Us* (Minneapolis: Interpersonal Communication Programs, Inc., 1981), 63-95.

[8] R.D. Hess and G. Handel, *Family World* (Chicago: University of Chicago Press, 1959).

its structure, including its power affiliations, its role definitions, and its relationship rules in order to be responsive to situational and cultural stresses."[9] Families live in a dynamic balance between being too structured (rigid) or too flexible (chaotic).

When a family is too structured, individual members are not open to change or to give input. The emphasis is on maintaining the *status quo* of relating and operating as family. Change is difficult and is faced with much resistance. When a family is too flexible, individual members are constantly exposed to unmitigated change. The structure is fluid and unstable, providing no sense of continuity. Family adaptability is worked out concretely by the family in the following issues:[10]

- *Leadership*. How and by whom is initiative taken?
- *Discipline*. How are limits set and consequences carried out?
- *Negotiations*. How are problems resolved?
- *Organization*. How organized is the family in accomplishing its tasks?
- *Values*. How are the values of the family determined and transmitted?

The following example, told by a young man, addresses family adaptability:

During one period of my childhood after my parents' divorce, my mother took a series of part-time jobs with variable hours, and my father left the state. My brother and I depended upon ourselves and the neighbors for whatever we needed. The family was very fragmented, and due to money and health problems, we never knew what would happen from day to day. After my mother seemed to straighten out her life a bit, we were able to do more things as a family and to get closer to each other again. Life was still pretty unpredictable. Finally, my mother married again, and we now live a very predictable life style, but it has allowed us to get closer to each other. We are a somewhat dull but close family.[11]

Each family develops a style of communication to work out the issues of cohesion and adaptability. The family and its members learn what may be communicated as well how to communicate it. Their style of communication can either facilitate or complicate the family's ability to be stable or to adapt and to bond or to be autonomous. As families address the issues of cohesion and adaptability, they establish a sense of their unique identity and discover how they want to be family at this particular time. In the beginning of a family's life, their identity can become cast in stone and be unable to adjust to the circumstances of new members and life.

Family of Origin

One's family of origin, the third dynamic of family systems, has a tremendous influence on the way one relates to his or her family of establishment or to significant social relationships. The family of origin refers to the original nuclear family (parents and siblings) plus relatives (grandparents, aunts, uncles, cousins). The influence of the family of origin is significant both in the past and the present. Parents themselves are someone's children, even as adults; they are still part of their own sibling system.

It is important to understand how one's own family of origin addressed the issues of cohesion and adaptability. Such understanding gives a family member insight into the emotional processes and patterns still at work in these relationships. Such understanding can also help persons modify their response to and aid significantly in the resolution of problems in both their immediate family and in their other relationships.

Recognizing the influence of one's family of origin is crucial to living together as a family:

. . . specific patterns of behavior, perceptions and thinking, as well as specific issues, for example, sex, money, territory, drinking, separation, health, have an uncanny way of reappearing. When family members are able to see beyond the horizons of their own nuclear family's area of trouble and observe the transmission of such issues from generation to generation, they often can obtain more distance from their immediate problems and, as a result, become freer to make changes.[12]

The patterns of relationship that one learns in his or her family of origin (e.g., mover/follower, bystander/resister, overfunctioner/underfunctioner) are the source of each person's uniqueness. Hence, it is also the starting point of one's ability to relate to other persons. Individuals seeking to change patterns of relationship first need to understand the influence of their family of origin on how they are relating at the present time. The role and position that they played in their family of origin will always have a major influence on how they relate to others.

This unique position can dilute or nourish natural strengths; it can be a dragging weight that slows our progress throughout life or an additive that enriches the mixture of our propelling fuel. The more one understands that position, therefore, and the more one can learn to occupy it with grace and "savvy," rather than fleeing from it or unwittingly allowing it to program our destiny, the more effectively one can function in other areas of our life.[13]

---

[9] *A New Design for Family Ministry*, 101.
[10] *Family Development I*, 25-59.
[11] D.H. Olson, et al., "Circumplex Model of Marital Systems: No. 1 Cohesion and Adaptability Dimension, Family Types and Clinical Application," *Family Process* 18:1 (March 1979).

[12] E. Friedman, *Generation to Generation: Family Process in Church and Synagogue* (New York: Guilford Press, 1985), 31-32.
[13] Ibid., 34.

Family Life Cycle

"Like every other living reality, the family too is called upon to develop and grow."[14] Just as each individual person continues to grow and develop a unique personality, so each family system continues to grow and develop a unique identity. This identity is greatly influenced by the quality of interaction of its members, its own developmental history, and predictable stages of development. These stages, the fourth dynamic of family systems, are called the family life cycle.

In each stage, a family has particular tasks to accomplish and challenges to face in order to prepare itself and its members for further growth and development. At each stage, a family and each of its members also have to readdress the issues of cohesion and adaptability. The structure that was developed at one particular time of the life cycle may need to be adjusted so that the family can more effectively function. "A new stage . . . is reached when (a person or married couple) is required to function in a new role, using information and skills that were not used or needed previously."[15] The family life cycle stages are:

1. *Establishment: new family without children.* This is the time for the newly married couple to become a separate, but connected unit of their extended family systems.
2. *New Parent(s): couple or one parent with one or more under-school-age child(ren).* This is the time when a new family moves to establish new subsystems: parent-child and sibling-sibling.
3. *School-Age Family: couple or one parent with school-age child(ren) and/or adolescents.* This is the time when a family needs to foster individuation and the growth of each of its members. This task frequently intensifies when children enter adolescence. At this time, the family needs to promote individuals' increasing independence while redefining family participation.
4. *Empty-Nest Family: couple or one parent during and after child(ren) leave home and/or enter the productive sector; middle-age couple without child(ren).* This is the time when a family begins to regroup and relate to each other and new members (in-laws) on an adult-to-adult basis.
5. *Aging Family: couple or one parent after retirement.* This is the time when a family deals with issues of retirement, death, role reversals, reinvestment, and diminishing financial and physical resources of the older members.

Today, individuals can be in different stages of the life cycle with different generations. For example, while individuals are members of their own family of origin, they can also have a family of establishment and be part of their children's and grandchildren's families.

---

[14] *Familiaris Consortio*, 65.
[15] *A New Design for Family Ministry*, 42.

Further, divorced and remarried persons often parent children of different stages from the current and previous marriages. Also, single adults go through life-cycle stages with their parents and their siblings.

Family Change

The fifth and final dynamic of family systems is change. A family is not a collection of individuals, but a living system of interdependent members. The changes that come into the lives of individual members affect all the family members as well as the family's roles and patterns of interaction. In order to monitor change so that it is not overwhelming or destructive to the family's functioning, each family has an unconscious, internal process that takes in information about itself and its members. This information helps a family determine whether to be open or closed to change. For some families, one more change may be unbearable, and for others, additional change may deepen the family's relationships.

Since change involves some loss, and loss is usually painful, families tend to resist change. The more fundamental the change, the greater will be the effect on the other members of a family. To change in response to another person is difficult. Change by one member challenges the roles and rules by which one's family operates, and causes stress that requires the family either to maintain its *status quo* or to adjust to the change.

When a family's internal process signals that change will threaten it, the family will seek to maintain the *status quo*. When this happens, the family addresses a changed member in one of a series of ways: (1) conscious or unconscious pressure is placed on the person to resume former roles, attitudes, values, or behavior; (2) the person is excluded or expelled from the inner life of the family; or (3) the family resigns itself to live with both the person and the tension that is caused, adapting and adjusting to the changes.

When a family seeks to adjust, the family's internal process signals that change is acceptable and needed for growth. When this happens, each member begins the process of changing in relation to the changed person, adjusting family roles and rules.

Ministry is designed to facilitate growth and conversion, which are forms of change. The discovery of God, the realization that life needs purpose, and entry into a believing community all involve real change. However, the way ministry is provided today frequently misses the systems aspects of an individual's change. Too often ministries fail to realize that the other members of a changing person's family are also affected. The effects of this change need serious attention.

Such attention is crucial not only for the family of the changing person, but for the individual as well, for the family has tremendous power over whether the person is able to integrate the new change. If the family has not supported and integrated the person into its system, it becomes harder for the person to retain the change and easier to regress to his or her previous ways of relating to self, others, and God.

The Roman Catholic Church in the United States currently makes extensive use of pastoral programs that precipitate change. These ministries seek to provide individuals with new attitudes, values, behaviors, and skills. The change precipitated in the family member may challenge the way a family operates. Yet, for the most part, the effects of these programs and processes on the family are not considered or addressed within these programs. Therefore, church leaders need to be aware that programs and ministries that actively seek to help participants live fuller Christian lives also affect the lives of the participants' families. These include:

- Intensive weekend experiences and ongoing ministerial programs, which seek to change or deepen attitudes, values, behaviors, and skills of the participants.
- The Rite of Christian Initiation of Adults and religious formation programs, which address the person's faith in a new way.
- Family life and sex education programs, which teach new knowledge, provide relationship skills, and address the values of the participants.
- Prayer and scripture groups for individuals, which often help move participants to a deeper experience and expression of prayer.
- Formal education programs (e.g., religious education, schools, campus ministry, adult education), which seek to root one's faith in the ongoing tradition and service of the Church, and which may challenge the participants to live differently.
- Parish renewal programs through which individuals become incorporated more deeply into the life of the parish.
- Formation programs for the priesthood, the permanent diaconate, religious life, and lay ministries, which involve entry into a new community of peers and ministry associates and, therefore, change the existing relationships with the trainee's family.
- Volunteer recruitment, training, and service for the various activities of the parish, diocese, or movements, which require adjustments in the time, energy, money, and activities of the volunteers' families.

These ministries and programs make positive contributions to the life of the Church and families. In many parishes and dioceses, they are a principal source of parish energy, staff, and volunteers. But they also cause individuals who participate in them to relate to their families in new ways, which at times can cause serious stress and confusion in their families. Therefore, church leaders need to help participants deal with the change within their families that these programs and ministries may induce. Further, it is important that leaders, together with the individual in the program, determine the following:

- How the individual's family is currently operating.
- How the individual's family addresses the issues of cohesion and adaptability.
- What roles the individual plays within his or her family, as well as the patterns of interaction.
- How open his or her family is to change.
- How the individual's change will affect his or her family and its members.
- What other family members would support the individual's change and help the family change its ways of relating and of assigning roles.
- What skills and knowledge may be needed by the family in order to change in response to the individual's change.

Family Impact Questions

To incorporate a family perspective that takes into account the element of the family as a developing system, leaders need to ask themselves questions such as the following about their specific policy, program, ministry, or service:

- How does it promote family strengths?
- In what ways does it address the individual's needs, the needs of the individual in relationship to his or her family, and the overall needs of the entire family?
- How does it determine whether there are competing needs within the family?
- How does it recognize the role family members play in contributing to or alleviating an individual's need for service?
- In what specific ways does it help individuals and families deal with changes the program may encourage?
- How does it direct itself to the needs of individuals and families at specific stages of the family life cycle?
- In what ways does it address multigenerational families? For example, a family with teenagers may also include a young adult who is beginning a family, as well as an aging and dependent grandparent(s).

tions, two-parent, single-parent, single-earner, dual-earner, childless, blended, and separated families. There is no longer a "typical" American family. Researchers speculate that three types of families with children have developed today in the United States: intact, single-parent, and blended.[1] Regardless of their structure, all families still have similar issues to deal with: to create their vision of family life, to grow as a family system, and to fulfill their own responsibilities in partnership with social institutions.

Norms

Despite the great variety in family structure, our culture still proposes that there is a typical or ideal kind of family. As a result, American families who do not resemble this ideal often feel inferior. Similarly, they may be treated differently by professionals in social institutions and, in effect, be penalized or judged pathological.

Issues

Families of different structures have to deal with stereotypes about themselves. For example, a single parent told this story:

> When my son Jimmy was in second grade, I began getting telephone calls from his teacher. She stated that while Jimmy wasn't experiencing any problems at the present time, she wanted to help me watch for any potential difficulties. I was perplexed. After a while, I finally realized what she was really getting at. A year previously, my husband and I had divorced. It was a difficult time for our family, but we really had worked hard so that both of us remained very involved with the children, and we watched the children adjust and go on with their lives. Jimmy's teacher, while meaning well, was evidently convinced that a child from a divorced or single-parent family had to experience school problems.

An anthropologist recently remarked that one of the historical anomalies of our time is that, as a culture, we focus on family structure, while the real issue today is family activities and responsibilities.[2] Although it will be difficult, our culture needs to shift its focus to the strengths and challenges inherent in each kind of family structure. For example, two-parent families have the strength of more adults to share family responsibilities; their challenge is that they suffer more from the myth that they should be self-sufficient. Single-parent families quickly realize they cannot make it alone and need the assistance of extended family members, friends, and others.

CHAPTER SIX
THE THIRD ELEMENT: FAMILY DIVERSITY

The first two elements of a family perspective—a Christian vision of family life and the family as a developing system—describe what families have in common. The third element of a family perspective provides insight into how families differ.

Each family is unique, and our pluralistic society is characterized by great diversity and changes in family life. Chapter One cited some statistics and trends as evidence of how family life is diverse. The point is that families in the United States differ greatly in their structure; in their special needs; in how they are affected by social trends; in their socioeconomic status; and in their cultural, ethnic, and religious heritages. This diversity can compliment or complicate the inner workings of family systems, not only because families have to deal with structural issues, social trends, cultural and religious issues, for example, but also because our society tends to *value* certain structures, economic status, ethnic and racial groups.

In order to understand this third element of a family perspective—family diversity—this manual takes five separate types of family diversity identified in Chapter One, looking at three aspects of each: (1) the range of *diversity* among families; (2) reflection on some operative social *norms*; and (3) some of the *issues* these diversities raise for families.

Family Structure

Diversity

Families come in many forms and configurations today: nuclear, extended, single or multiple genera-

---

[1] A. Cherlin, *The Diversity and Strength of American Families*, 40.
[2] H. Varenne, "The Family: A Modern Anthropological Perspective," *Families and Television: A Book of Readings* (Washington, D.C.: The National Center for Family Studies at The Catholic University of America, 1987).

Special Needs

Diversity

All families experience developmental changes over the course of their life cycle (see Chapter Four). For example, as children move from grade school to adolescence, and adults move from parenting to pre-retirement, families may need additional supports to make these changes. Many families, however, have special needs and face difficult problems, which may be developmental, critical, or chronic.

In fact, most families face crises and emergencies at different times in their life together: for example, a death in the family, a sudden illness, the birth of a disabled child, a divorce, an elderly parent developing Alzheimer's disease, or unemployment. These special needs may be short-term or may become chronic (e.g., an illness could become a disability), and often they require the support of family, friends, and community services.

Norms

Unfortunately, most American families still live with the myth, inherited from their agricultural ancestors, that families are completely self-reliant and should be able to take care of all their needs themselves. Further, the myth maintains that families should be places of love and warmth and should be essentially problem-free. This pressures families to keep special needs and problems (e.g., marital conflicts) hidden and to turn to others for help only reluctantly and then only if shrouded in confidentiality.

Issues

When a special need arises, families have to understand how vitally it affects the family. Clearly, a crisis is bound to change how the family system operates. A mother told the following story:

Family life is incredibly subtle and complex. Everything seems tied to everything else, and it's very difficult to sort out what is going on. For example, when our oldest daughter Marcy contracted spinal meningitis, the whole family reflected the strain. My second daughter and I fought more, while my husband tended to withdraw into himself, which brought me closer to my son. In their own ways, the three children became closer while our marriage became more distant. As Marcy's recovery progressed, there were more changes, which affected how we relate now, two years later. That one event highlighted the difficulty of sorting out what is really going on.[3]

Families also have to learn how to get help when they experience a special need. Unfortunately, our society still focuses almost exclusively on a remedial approach: families seek help *after* a crisis has occurred and other problems develop. An alternate is a preventive strategy. The following story of a family who did not deal well with a death crisis is a good—if sad—example of society's remedial approach to problems:

A father reported that he was a blue-collar worker whose wife had died from cancer. After a long illness which drained the family's financial and emotional resources, this man sought assistance to keep his family together. He discovered that his $15,000 annual salary, modest by today's standards, was too high for government support and too low to pay for private housekeeping and child care. The pressures of keeping his family together intensified, and he turned to alcohol. He lost his job, and the family strains grew worse. Finally, the community responded to his problem by taking his kids away and placing them in foster homes while he obtained help with his alcoholism. The government, which could not provide modest assistance, was now paying $45,000 annually for foster care and juvenile detention.[4]

Social Trends

Diversity

Families are also affected by certain trends in society, such as mobility and migration, the emphasis on individualism and self-fulfillment, the employment of both or the only parent, the aging of America, divorce, the sexual revolution, and the women's movement.

Norms

Americans manifest a marked ambivalence about most of these social trends. But no matter the reactions these trends elicit, the fact remains they raise serious concerns, and each family must come to terms with them.

Take, for example, sex roles and their relationship with the world of work:

Changing norms of what a woman is "supposed to do" as wife and mother and what a man is supposed to do as husband and father are transforming the institutions of the workplace and the family. Probably no set of shifting norms carry greater significance for the culture. Norms affecting whether a wife should work outside the home have, within a single generation, reversed themselves. It should be kept in mind that some women in America have always worked outside the home. The number of working women has increased in recent years, but the phenomenon is not novel. What is new is the cultural meaning of women working. In the eighteenth century, and particularly in the nineteenth, it was not unusual for the whole family—the husband, his wife, and his children—to

---

[3] *Family Communication*, 27.

[4] The *Washington Star*, (June, 1980).

work for pay outside the home. In the late nineteenth and early twentieth centuries, as the nation industrialized and wealth grew, it became a source of pride for a man to be so successful as a provider that this children and even his wife no longer had to work outside the home. In the early post-World War II years, the majority of women with children who worked were blue-collar, not blue-stocking. When middle-class women worked outside the home, a clear understanding existed between the husband and wife. Even if the wife earned as much as or more than the husband, the norm insisted that rent and food money come from his salary. It was acceptable to use the wife's income for "extras," to pay for a housecleaner once or twice a week, or a baby-sitter, or even a vacation, but not for the necessities of life. . . . Happily or unhappily, the dual-earner family is rapidly becoming the norm, now accounting for a majority of households. Although economic need pushes many women to paid jobs, it is not easy to define economic need. In many families, husbands and wives both work to maintain a standard of living that they have come to enjoy and expect, though they hardly "need" it in a literal sense. Indeed, an impressive 67% of women who work say that they do so for self-fulfillment reasons as well as economic ones.[5]

Even women who opt to stay home to be full-time mothers feel pressure in the form of a subtle prejudice that insinuates that to have any meaning or purpose in life everyone must have a paying job. Parenting is placed on a part-time basis.

These changes raise real and serious issues for families, particularly in defining sex roles and the meaning and purpose of family life. One writer, summarizing the changes for women, puts it this way:

> The [cultural] message [of an earlier America] said: serve your husband and children; subordinate your desires to theirs; be a good mother, wife and hostess; be passive, gracious and feminine—and your husband will take care of you. . . . The new cultural message said: it is acceptable for you to have what successful men have—desires of your own; opportunities for self-expression, independence and recognition; actions on your own behalf; exercise of control over your own life; and pursuit of a career that does not force you to hide your intelligence behind "feminine" wiles. . . . How to preserve warmth and closeness while at the same time holding onto the new freedom to choose?— this is the preeminent question the culture confronts on the domestic scene.[6]

Issues

The following, related by a woman, is an example of the effects of the employment of both parents on a family:

> I made a decision to go back to work to help cover the bills. I had a six-month, unpaid child care leave, and if I didn't return, I would have lost my job. In order to go back to work, my husband and I had to make serious adjustments in our family life. My husband

agreed to assist in household chores, and we developed a format for co-parenting our children. Because of the job demands, travel to and from work, time spent transporting children, we have had to be creative with time arrangements, personal space, family involvements, and our personal relationships. Going from 5:30 a.m. to 10:00 p.m. with two full-time jobs leaves little time during the week for anything else, and at times really causes stress in our marriage.

Economic Status

Diversity

Families are also diverse in their socioeconomic status, which affects their ability to maintain their unity, health, well-being, and stability. The range includes the poor, the lower middle class, the middle class, the upper middle class, and the rich.

Poverty among families with children in the United States is increasing, not decreasing. Most vulnerable are the unemployed, the unemployable, the underemployed, and those whose employment is threatened;[7] ". . . burdens fall most heavily on blacks, Hispanics, and native Americans. Even more disturbing is the large increase in the number of women and children living in poverty. Today, children are the largest single group among the poor."[8] Official poverty statistics number 35 million Americans as poor, even after government money transfers (welfare, social security, etc.). The number would approach 60 million in the absence of such programs.[9]

Further, many working people and middle-class Americans live dangerously close to poverty. "A rising number of families must rely on the wages of two or even three members just to get by. From 1968 to 1978, nearly a quarter of the U.S. population was in poverty part of the time and received welfare benefits in at least one year. The loss of a job, illness, or the breakup of a marriage may be all it takes to push people into poverty."[10] Public opinion polls reveal that "the near-poor, hard-working, salaried Americans believe their security—the fruits of their own work, their savings, and their loyalty to society's rules—is being undermined by inflation, taxes, and chicanery. Millions of middle-income Americans—home-owning, dual-earner families—feel they are on a treadmill or adrift in a dangerous world with inadequate [economic] leadership."[11] It is not surprising, then, that "many middle-class Americans feel themselves in the grip of

---

[5] *New Rules: Searching for Self-Fulfillment*, 98-99, 101.
[6] Ibid., 65, 103

[7] P. Voydanoff, "The Church and Economically Distressed Families," *Families, the Economy, and the Church: A Book of Readings and Discussion Guide* (Washington, D.C.: USCC Office of Publishing and Promotion Services, 1987).
[8] *Economic Justice for All*, 16.
[9] P. Schervish, "Family Life and the Economy: Graver Responsibilities and Scarcer Resources," *Families, the Economy, and the Church.*
[10] *Economic Justice for All*, 17.
[11] *New Rules: Searching for Self-Fulfillment*, 212-213.

economic demands and cultural pressures that go far beyond the individual family's capacity to cope."[12]

The reality is that economic factors are the greatest stressor of family life, among all income levels. This is true for both low-income and high-income families; the stressors merely change.[13]

Norms

By looking at the expectations people have about their economic situation, one can discover that the central normative issue regarding economic status is the unconscious agreement that people believe they have made to attain their status. One observer of American culture describes this agreement in the following way:

> In the 40's and 50's, individuals operated on the following: I give hard work, loyalty and steadfastness. I swallow my frustrations and suppress my impulse to do what I would enjoy, and do what is expected of me instead. I do not put myself first; I put the needs of others ahead of my own. I give a lot, but what I get in return is worth it. I receive an ever-growing standard of living, and a family life with a devoted spouse and decent kids. Our children will take care of us in our old age if we really need it, which thank goodness we will not. I have a nice home, a good job, the respect of my friends and neighbors; a sense of accomplishment at having made something of my life. Last but not least, as an American I am proud to be a citizen of the finest country in the world.
>
> In the 60's and 70's, individuals added onto the traditional demands for material well-being new demands for intangibles—creativity, leisure, autonomy, pleasure, participation, community, adventure, vitality, stimulation, tender loving care. To the efficiency of technological society they wish to add joy of living.[14]

Unfortunately, there are some serious problems with these unconscious or perceived agreements. First, this agreement is based on a false premise: namely, that each person will continue to advance economically. In fact, however, "the promise of economic advancement beyond that of our own parents has collapsed."[15] Real family income has not increased since 1973.

Second, the agreement is based on a psychology of affluence that is pervasive in our culture, one that insists that "we do not need to choose, we have a right to more."[16] It has four features:

1. [The psychology of affluence's] most prominent feature is [this] mentality: the expectation of a high material standard of living *and* clean air, water, and other environmental protections *and* affirmative action programs for the disadvantaged *and* protection against illness, unemployment, old age, and other

life risks *and* the full rich life built around leisure, self-expression, and personalized life styles. This is the familiar "we expect-more-of-everything" outlook.
2. A second feature of the psychology of affluence assumes that acquiring more of everything is a matter of personal entitlement rather than a mere hope or desire.
3. Its third characteristic is to take for granted that the economy will function more or less automatically. The economy is Big Mother, indestructible and bountiful, though sometimes she won't respond unless one screams and yells.
4. A fourth feature . . . is that it turns the self-denial ethic on its head. Instead of a concern with moral obligations to others pursued at the cost of personal desire, we have the concept of duty to self pursued at the cost of moral obligations to others. Personal desire achieves the status of an ethical norm.[17]

Issues

The bishops' pastoral letter on the economy, *Economic Justice for All,* speaks to one of the grave issues raised by the question of economic status:

> The lack of a mutually supportive relation between family life and economic life is one of the most serious problems facing the United States today. The economic and cultural strength of the nation is directly linked to the stability and health of its families. When families thrive, spouses contribute to the common good through their work at home, in the community, and in their jobs; and children develop a sense of their own worth and of their responsibility to serve others. When families are weak or break down entirely, the dignity of parents and children is threatened. High cultural and economic costs are inflicted on society at large.[18]

Thus, one economic issue many families in our nation face is what happens to them when the economy fails them. For example, when a major industry shuts down and hundreds of employees are thrown out of work, the results are far reaching.

> I spoke with the pastor of a church in a community that suffered severe economic depression when an automotive plant closed. He expressed dismay at the disruption it caused within family life. "If you told me a year ago that some of these strong families were only as strong as the breadwinner's weekly paycheck, I would have disagreed," he said. "But now I realize how fragile and dependent families are upon the economy."[19]

Another issue families face is coming to terms with the impact of the psychology of affluence on family values. As the bishops' pastoral letter on the economy states:

> . . . A large number of women and men, drawing on their religious tradition, recognize the challenging vo-

---

[12] *Economic Justice for All,* 23.

[13] D. Curran, *Stress and the Healthy Family* (New York: Harper and Row, 1985).

[14] *New Rules: Searching for Self-Fulfillment,* 7.

[15] "Family Life and the Economy," *Families, the Economy, and the Church.*

[16] *New Rules: Searching for Self-Fulfillment,* 211.

[17] Ibid., 186-187.

[18] *Economic Justice for All,* 18.

[19] *Stress and the Healthy Family,* 11.

cation of family life and child rearing in a culture that emphasizes material display and self-gratification. . . .

. . . Together we must reflect on our personal and family decisions and curb unnecessary wants in order to meet the needs of others. There are many questions we must keep asking ourselves: Are we becoming ever more wasteful in a "throw-away" society? Are we able to distinguish between our true needs and those thrust on us by advertising and a society that values consumption more than saving? . . .

Husbands and wives, in particular, should weigh their needs carefully and establish a proper priority of values. . . .[20]

Similarly, the bishops also challenge families to ask themselves basic questions about the nature of our economic system:

. . . does our economic system place more emphasis on maximizing profits than on meeting human needs and fostering human dignity? Does our economy distribute its benefits equitably or does it concentrate power and resources in the hands of a few? Does it promote excessive materialism and individualism? Does it adequately protect the environment and the nation's natural resources? Does it direct too many scarce resources to military purposes? . . .[21]

Cultural, Ethnic, and Religious Heritages

Diversity and Norms

The United States is the most ethnically diverse nation in the world. Virtually every ethnic, racial, and religious group is represented in our nation. Nevertheless, every nation has its own culture, even one characterized by great diversity like our own. Culture can be defined as "the values, shared meanings, social norms, customs, rituals, symbols, arts and artifacts, ways of perceiving the world, life styles, behaviors, and ideologies by which people participate in an organized society."[22] A culture passes on its values primarily through socialization in families.

The United States has a dominant culture, one promoted by the most well-established groups. This dominant culture stresses a value system with a future orientation, mastery over nature, the mixed good-bad nature of humans, doing as opposed to being, and individuality.[23] The dominant culture tends to devalue those other groups, which do not promote these values in their families.

The tension between the ideals of family behavior imposed by the dominant culture and the traditional patterns of ethnic groups has been a recurring issue in American life. The first imposed solution to this tension was the "melting pot" process that promoted

. . . a tendency toward homogenization of American culture and, with it, an increasing emphasis on uniformity in family behavior. Immigrants, primarily in the second generation, adapted their family size, withdrawal of wives from the labor force, and changing styles of consumption and tastes. However, this ongoing process did not result in a total assimilation of family ways and traditional customs, because new waves of immigrants have tended to bring with them (other) family patterns.

It is therefore unrealistic to talk simply about *the* American family. Until very recently, the stereotype of the private nuclear family as the ideal family in American society has been dominant. Alternative forms of family organization, such as those of various ethnic families, were misinterpreted as "family disorganization" because they did not conform to the official stereotype. But actually over the past decade, the strength and resilience of ethnic families has been recognized. These traditional resources of family and kinship among certain ethnic groups have been rediscovered . . . and (ethnic family diversity) is now being valued as a source of strength and continuity, rather than being described as a manifestation of deviance.[24]

Issues

Thus, for many families, the values and traditions inherent in their ethnic and religious heritage are a source of family strength. For example, many black families' strengths come from these roots.

One of the traditional and continuing stress-absorbing systems for Black families has been the wider supportive network of their families. These reciprocal exchange systems have enabled Blacks to cope with, and sometimes transcend, severe environmental stress. These networks extend beyond the house to include relatives of several generations. They often include friends and church members who become as a family or *fictive kin*.

The extended family-help system, the "elasticity" of family boundaries, the high level of informal adoption, and the important supportive role of religious groups, have augmented existing internal family supports in being able to cope with stress. The wider extended families are a source of emotional and instrumental strength, especially during periods of high stress. The "kin insurance policies" were very active because goods and services flow in both directions between mobile and nonmobile family members.[25]

Many black leaders today, however, indicate that these strengths are being eroded by the impact of unemployment.

One special need facing many families today is immigration and migration, which is particularly stress-

[20] *Economic Justice for All*, 2, 334-335.

[21] Ibid., 132.

[22] F. Kluckhohn, "Variations in the Basic Values of Family Systems," *A Modern Introduction to the Family* (New York: Basic Books, 1968).

[23] Haraven, *The Diversity and Strength of American Families*, 39.

[24] Ibid.

[25] H. P. McAdoo, "Afro-American Families: An Element of Actualization," *Families: Black and Catholic, Catholic and Black*, Sr. T. Bowman, FSPA, Ph.D., ed. (Washington, D.C.: USCC Office of Publishing and Promotion Services, 1985), 27.

ful for families who flee their homeland to escape persecution. The following story illustrates the impact of immigration on a family, and the resulting clash in cultural values:

We left our village in El Salvador in 1983: three children and two adults. Our first stop was Guatemala, where we remained a number of weeks with family members; then came Mexico City and eventually Los Angeles, also for short stays with relatives or one-time fellow villagers; and finally, Washington, D.C., where many of our fellow villagers from El Salvador now live, and where one of us got a job in a restaurant. Four cities, three countries, and a job without totally leaving behind our neighbors, family ties, familiar language, or shared cultural symbols. Each new stop partook so much of the village we left behind that, in many ways, our new life was a continuation of the old, but with many frightening new additions. Once settled in Washington, we did our best to keep our old ways, but the children want to be like all the other Americans. Ironically, this is going on at the same time we may be forced to choose between remaining illegal aliens in this country or returning to El Salvador.

It is not only immigrant families who face clashes between the dominant culture and their ethnic family values. One of the major themes of Hispanics in the Catholic Church in the United States is the beauty and strength of Hispanic family values, the fear of assimilation, and finally, what Hispanic family values can contribute to American culture.[26] This same issue is faced by other ethnic groups such as the Vietnamese and others.

Another issue that faces many families today is what happens when cultures and religions are mixed through marriage. One man told the following story:

I was raised in a German, Catholic farm community in Nebraska. When I was a kid, one of my uncles married a Catholic girl who was Polish. My family, indignant, finally accepted the situation, and to save face, called it a "mixed marriage." Twenty years later, of my six married siblings, three are married to Catholics, one to a Mormon, one to a born-again fundamentalist, and one to a Buddhist. My siblings and their spouses are dealing with issues such as "What religious values do we teach our children?" "What rituals and symbols can

we express in the household?" The kids ask, "Why can't the whole family go to communion?" These may seem like easy questions, but they are the source of a lot of disagreements, confusion, pain, hard work, and joy in my family.

Family Impact Questions

To incorporate a family perspective that takes into account the element of family diversity, leaders need to ask themselves questions such the following about their specific policy, program, ministry, or service:

- Which of the aspects of family diversity described in this chapter are evident in the participating families? What are the implications for the policy or program?
- Describe the different kinds of family structures manifested by persons who participate in the program. What are the implications for the program?
- Describe how it addresses families with special needs. How does it seek to support these families in both preventive and remedial ways?
- In what specific ways does it help families deal with the tensions of changing sex roles? What adjustments are needed in the policy or program to ensure that they take these new roles into account?
- How does it help families deal with the social trends that affect their life together (e.g., mobility, individualism and self-fulfillment, the employment of both parents or the only parent, the aging of America, divorce)?
- In what specific ways do present personnel policies within the organization affect the family life of employees? What adjustments need to be made?
- Does it direct itself toward a specific socioeconomic group? Is this justified?
- In what ways is it directed toward specific groups who need special help but are not receiving it (e.g., the unemployed, the unemployable, and the underemployed)?[27]
- How is it specifically adjusted to individuals and families of different ethnic and religious heritages? What further adjustments need to be made?
- How does it help intercultural or ecumenical families form their own unique vision of family life?

[26] National Conference of Catholic Bishops, *The Hispanic Presence: Challenge and Commitment*, Pastoral Letter of the U.S. Bishops (Washington, D.C.: USCC Office of Publishing and Promotion Services, 1983).

[27] "The Church and Economically Distressed Families," *Families, the Economy, and the Church.*

CHAPTER SEVEN
THE FOURTH ELEMENT:
THE PARTNERSHIP BETWEEN FAMILIES AND SOCIAL INSTITUTIONS

Change has always been a part of family life, but the degree and rapidity of change affecting family life today is unusual. This rapidity, however, does not mean that these changes are unrecognizable or random. What they are, where they have come from, and why they are taking place can be described.

In all cultures, the family has been the basic agency for performing important tasks, from preparing for the birth of children to helping the elderly die. Today, however, we are experiencing changes in family responsibilities, for example, in child care and health care. For the most part, the changes reflect a sharing of responsibilities between families and specialized institutions:

> Historians agree that the most crucial change wrought by industrialization was the transfer of functions from the family to other institutions. The preindustrial family served as a workshop, church, reformatory, school, and asylum. Over the past century and a half, these functions have become in large part the responsibility of other institutions. The household has been transfomed form a place of production to a place of consumption and for nurturing children. The family has withdrawn from the world of work, extolling privacy and intimacy as its major sources of strength, and the workplace has generally become nonfamilial and bureaucratic.[1]

Many people find this sharing or their responsibilities difficult, partly because it runs counter to what

they are accustomed to, partly because it does not fit their expectations of family life.

Consequently, the fourth element that enters into forming and implementing a family perspective is the need to establish a working relationship, a partnership between families and those institutions that now share the responsibilities once held by families. The lack of such a partnership accounts for much of the stress that families face today. For example, parents and teachers might see each other as rivals in the education of children, or doctors and families regard each other as obstacles in their desire to help an ill member.

Changes in family responsibilities have occurred as the nation moved from its agricultural roots. The so-called traditional or agricultural-based family was typical in the United States well into the nineteenth century. The industrial family structure, which dominated in the late nineteenth century, remains with us today but is giving way to today's families who are living in a technological, information society. The three sections that follow indicate that family life truly has changed and point out specific areas of change; it is a somewhat simplified version of a rather complicated development. Following this explication, the implications of these changes for social policy and social institutions are discussed.

The Family in Agricultural Society

In agricultural society, the family itself was *the* social institution in which important responsibilities were met. Both men and women worked for the family and received their financial support from the family's efforts, either on their own land or as laborers working for someone else. The family taught people their roles, their crafts, and their prayers. If people fell sick, the family took care of them. If they stepped out of line, family members called them to account. Recreation took place at family and kin celebrations. Spouses were chosen or approved by the family, and when people died, the family buried them. The family in agricultural society, therefore, had the following responsibilities: (1) economic support (unit of production); (2) employment; (3) health and mental-health care; (4) education and socialization; (5) social control; (6) religion; (7) recreation; (8) marrying; (9) reproduction; (10) identity, affection, and love; and (11) protective care of children, the frail, the disabled, and the chronically ill.

This arrangement did not mean that family life was always easy or successful in agricultural families. At its best, people belonged to caring systems and had a clear sense of identity. At its worst, individual needs were not recognized because the families' needs dominated; individuals, frequently women and children, were abused.

---

[1] T. Haraven, "Themes in the Historical Development of the Family," *The Family: Review of Child Development Research*, vol. 7, ed. Parke (Chicago: University of Chicago Press, 1984), 171.

The Family in Industrial Society

As society industrialized, it required smaller and more mobile families, and hence fewer household members to help in meeting responsibilities. Thus, the majority of the family's previously held responsibilities began to be shared with institutions. There were now schools for education, hospitals for the sick, mills and factories for employment, and a police force for the unruly. In the Church, with the promulgation of the Baltimore Catechism, religious education became centralized, and piety became parish-based. Services once provided within the family itself were now being shared or taken over by people especially trained for particular services rendered. This left industrial families with fewer responsibilities that were solely their own.

Some argue that the appearance of these institutions deprived the family of its role in caring for its own members. However, the evidence seems to argue that these services became institutionalized precisely because the family no longer was able to exclusively shoulder all its previous responsibilities. The ability of the family authority to bring the members together to meet a need or threat was lessened because the role of the head was diffused. In industrial employment, individual family members also were able to contract individually for their services. This gave them more personal independence and lessened family control. But no matter the cause of the rise of these institutions, the effect was to leave industrial families with fewer responsibilities that were solely their own.

In industrial society, the individual still looked to the family for social security during long-term illness or unemployment. However, the definition of family became more restricted. Whereas the family once included an extended kin network (whether they lived in the same household or not—the later being more often the case), and on the farm, might even include retainers or boarders, the family was fast becoming restricted to the household structure, with extended kin more scattered.

Recreation remained family-focused. Marrying, reproduction, and the rearing of preschool children were still in the hands of the family. Thus, the family began to specialize in child rearing and in maintaining the home as a private retreat from the outside world. However, the choice of a spouse had shifted from the family into the hands of the individual.

Families in industrial society could claim the following responsibilities as theirs alone: (1) economic support (unit of consumption of goods and services); (2) recreation; (3) marrying; (4) reproduction; (5) identity, affection, and love; and (6) protective care of children, the frail, the disabled, and the chronically ill.

The Family in Technological Society

From the mid-1950s on, major changes have occurred in American life. These changes have drawn the center of action and responsibility away from the family. The following examples indicate this tendency:

- The federal government, with its social welfare programs such as Aid to Families with Dependent Children (AFDC), social security, Medicare, Supplemental Security Income (SSI), and local government support in other emergencies, have made government the source of ultimate financial security in crisis situations.
- Television, which is the principal recreation for Americans, is a solitary form of recreation and socialization. Leisure-time industries, of increasing economic significance, compete for the remainder of Americans' free time.
- With the development of computers and the subsequent knowledge explosion, families are increasingly reliant on information drawn from outside the home.
- In the Catholic parish, marrying is now regulated by diocesan policies that move the preparation into the hands of professionals.[2]
- The typical family now relies on child care rather than having the children cared for solely at home.

Clearly, the families in a technological society have fewer responsibilities solely within their domain. In fact, only two major responsibilities are exclusively theirs: (1) reproduction; and (2) identity, affection, and love.

The rest of the responsibilities that once constituted family life are now shared with a variety of institutions. This points up dramatically how much and how fast family life has changed in recent years. Those who grew up on American farms and who now live in cities could have witnessed all these changes.

To demonstrate the great shift of responsibilities from families to institutions, the changes are listed side by side in Chart 1, below.

Transfer of Responsibilities

As noted above, many family responsibilities have been transferred to institutions or are now shared with institutions. This transfer/sharing still continues; the

---

[2] *Preparing for Marriage.*

Chart 1: Families' Sole Responsibilities In:

Agricultural Society	Industrial Society	Technological Society
1. Economic support	1. Economic support	1. Reproduction
2. Employment	2. Recreation	2. Identity, affection, love
3. Health and mental health care	3. Marrying	
4. Education and socialization	4. Reproduction	
5. Social control	5. Identity, affection, love	
6. Religion	6. Some protective care of children, the frail, the disabled, the chronically ill	
7. Recreation		
8. Marrying		
9. Reproduction		
10. Identity, affection, love		
11. Protective care of children, the frail, the disabled, the chronically ill		

growing number of children now in child care is but one of the most common examples. For the sake of illustration, the institutionalized responsibilities are listed in Chart 2, below.

New Family Responsibilities

This transfer does not tell the whole story of family responsibilities by any means. Even though institutions *provide* services, families are still primarily responsible for these human needs. An example may help to explain: if a family member becomes seriously ill, the family is still responsible for getting the person the medical treatment he or she needs, whether they live in the same household or not. At the same time, this responsibility can tax seriously the ill person's family, financially and emotionally, even with reliance on the health care system for assistance.

Likewise, families have also taken on *new* responsibilities, all of them oriented to coping with the new social situation (see Chart 3, below). The industrial family took on the new responsibility of coordinating the family's use of institutional services, and this responsibility has expanded for today's technological family. Finding the appropriate service and a humane service provider, and getting family members to the

Chart 2: Responsibilities Shared between Families and Institutions

Agricultural Society	Industrial Society	Technological Society
1. Limited sharing	1. Employment	1. Employment
	2. Health and mental health care	2. Health and mental health care
	3. Education and socialization	3. Education and socialization
	4. Social control	4. Social control
	5. Religion	5. Religion
		6. Some recreation
		7. Marrying
		8. Some childcare
		9. Protective care of children, the frail, the disabled, the chronically ill

Chart 3: New Responsibilities Taken on by Families

Industrial Society	Technological Society
1. Coordination of services	1. Coordination of services 2. Reliance on services, goods, and information 3. Greater emphasis on love, affection, and greater need for protective care of surviving members

many institutions for service is hard enough; integrating them is even more difficult.

Since the technological family has taken on the responsibility to coordinate services, much more is demanded. This new responsibility reflects the major place of consumerism in family life, the family's increased reliance on services, and its ever-increasing need for information. Families today expend tremendous amounts of energy and income in obtaining services and getting information.

Also, the role of love, affection, and protective care in the family has taken on a new importance due both to the greater rate of survival of family members and to privatization of family life. Almost all children survive to adulthood, which is the greatest change, and adults survive to an older age; families have more surviving members today who must be cared for when frail, disabled, or chronically ill. Further, families today have the highest expectations in the history of civilization of what marriage and family life emotionally will provide their members, with a concomitant emphasis on the privacy of the home. As a result, the climate of emotional support takes on a prominence it did not have previously.

Applications to Social Institutions

Even though social institutions now share many of families' responsibilities, they can never totally usurp families' responsibilities. Families are never to become bit players in their relationships with their own members. Families' responsibilities cannot be replicated by institutions without an incredible social and financial cost. Economic support and basic welfare, health and mental-health care, education and socialization, social control, recreation, reproduction, formation of identity, affection, and nurturance are all basic responsibilities of families. Can one imagine a society where families did not provide them? Thus, it is in society's best interest to enter into creative partnerships with families so that families can fulfill these responsibilities. Families are the key to improving the educational success of children; they are crucial for planning and delivering care for the frail elderly; they remain the

essential resource helping those who are in trouble. Accordingly, it is crucial to society that its institutions (which include employment and service institutions, the Church, and the government—as reflected in public policy) enter into strong partnerships with families.

1. Employment and Service Institutions

Employment institutions need to realize that in the two-parent family where both parents are employed, and in the one-parent household where the only parent is employed, people experience tremendous pressures trying to balance the demands of family life and work. There are some employers who are experimenting with methods to help balance these demands (e.g., flex-time, child care, cafeteria-style benefits, etc.). A truly serious consideration of these innovations will come about only if employers join with families in realizing that family well-being is not just the family's issue, but is an issue that also affects productivity in the workplace.

Service institutions, too, need to reevaluate their relationships with families. For example, some hospitals limit family visits. This practice implies that the presence of the family will impede rather than help the patient's recovery. Experience and studies show that family support assists recovery. A partnership between family members and medical personnel would seem to be a great asset in patient recovery.[3]

Likewise, schools share with families the task of educating children. Reports indicate, however, that parents often expect teachers to provide moral formation and social skills in accord with the parents' views as well as to provide educational instruction. The implication is that the parents are expecting too much of the school system. Teachers, in turn, expect parents to support them in educating the child, but not to interfere in that education. The implication is that the teachers expect too little educational competence from the parents. A partnership recognizes both the need of parents and teachers to work together

---

[3] S. Farkis, *Hospitalized Children: The Family's Role in Their Care and Treatment* (Washington, D.C.: The National Center for Family Studies at The Catholic University of America, 1984).

in all aspects of education and the complementary roles of parents and teachers.[4]

In these three areas—employment, health care, and education—and in other areas as well, responsibilities have now shifted from families to specialized institutions. The American respect for progress could lead to the assumption that this transfer was not only inevitable but an improvement. But analysis shows that the institutionalization of these responsibilities has exacted a high price. Individuals and society are not better served by excluding families from participation in these services to their members.

2. The Church

The Church, like employment and service organizations, works with families in fulfilling some basic family responsibilities, such as education, support, religious and value formation, socialization, religious practice, health care, and social services. The Church is also very much involved in social issues of direct importance to families, such as economics and nuclear armaments.

Consequently, the Church must address the issue of its partnership with families. The principles that apply to social institutions and to social policy apply to the Church as well. What the Church does and how it does it affects the unity, well-being, health, and stability of families. Church leaders need to be more aware of how the Church's policies, programs, ministries, and services can either help or hinder families in fulfilling their own basic responsibilities. Church leaders need to see themselves as partners with families, and they need to resist the tendency—common in service institutions—to replace or substitute for families in fulfilling family responsibilities.

3. The Government and Social Policy

Besides employment and service organizations and the Church, the changes in families also have affected the partnership that exists between families and the government, as reflected in public social policy. The bishops' pastoral letter on the economy states: "In the principle of subsidiarity, Catholic social teaching has long stressed the importance of small- and intermediate-sized communities or institutions in exercising moral responsibility. These mediating structures link the individual to society as a whole in a way that gives people greater freedom and power to act."[5] The family as a mediating structure needs to play a crucial role with society in the pursuit of the public good.

When families are working well, they carry out responsibilities essential for the functioning of society. When families are in trouble, the government must often act in their place. The government then establishes remedial programs for individuals in trouble, but at tremendous cost. Perhaps such trouble frequently could be prevented if all institutions worked to support family strengths and to develop services for individuals, which take families into account.

The reason government policies and programs deserve specific attention when discussing partnerships between families and institutions is because they often set the direction for institutional services. And even more fundamental, the role of government in family life is becoming pervasive. Today, government policies and services have a tremendous effect on the functioning of families. They provide vital and essential supports for families to help them fulfill their basic responsibilities. Even a decade ago, over 200 government programs had a direct or indirect impact on family life.[6]

It is important that the government keep in constant dialogue with families so that it does not exclude or marginalize families through its policies. *Familiaris Consortio* states:

The family and society have complementary functions in defending and fostering the good of each and every human being. But society—more specifically the state—must recognize that "the family is a society in its own right," and so society is under a grave obligation in its relations with the family to adhere to the principle of subsidiarity.

By virtue of this principle, the state cannot and must not take away from families the functions that they can just as well perform on their own or in free associations; instead it must positively favor and encourage as far as possible responsible initiatives by families. In the conviction that the good of the family is an indispensable and essential value of the civil community, the public authorities must do everything possible to ensure that families have all those aids—economic, social, educational, political, and cultural assistance—that they need in order to face all their responsibilities in a human way.[7]

A fuller explication of the rights of the family is presented in the *Charter of the Rights of the Family*, developed by the Holy See.[8] This Charter expresses fundamental parameters for legislation from a family perspective. When legislation attacks or does not defend these basic rights, the way of life of the family and, therefore, society is at stake. These rights can be

. . . categorized as either developmental, environmental, or political. All statements of rights are political in one sense, and these categories are not, in the strictest sense, mutually exclusive. But the following categorization can help us to think about the path to the fullest implementation of [family] rights.

The developmental rights, namely, family establishment, procreation, right to life, socialization, intimacy, stability, and worthy elderly existence, are the very

---

[4] A. T. Henderson et al., *Beyond the Bake Sale: An Educator's Guide to Working with Parents* (Columbia, Md.: National Committee for Citizens in Education, 1986).

[5] *Economic Justice for All*, 308.

[6] Family Impact Seminar, *Toward an Inventory of Federal Programs with Direct Impact on Families* (Washington, D.C.: The Family Impact Seminar, 1978).

[7] *Familiaris Consortio*, 45.

[8] *Charter of the Rights of the Family* (Washington, D.C.: USCC Office of Publishing and Promotion Services, 1983).

foundation of the family as a family. A compromise on any of these strike at the very heart of the family and its *raison d'etre*.

Whatever the particular organizational form of the family, the environment and political rights serve and support the developmental rights. Housing, recreation, security, and protection from unwanted external corruptions—these enhance socialization, intimacy, stability, and the worthiness of the elderly's existence. The formation of associations, the support of free expression and representation, the respect for traditions, and the practice of faith and ultimately immigration, are often means necessary to the improvement or even basic actualization of environmental and developmental rights.[9]

Governmental social policy that supports family rights is needed because "families' lives and government are not independent of each other but deeply intertwined."[10] The more explicit these policies are, the less it is possible for them to usurp family responsibilities or to burden families unnecessarily as they carry out their responsibilities. This is a difficult goal to achieve because

> . . . most government programs have been either designed for individuals oblivious of their family roles and responsibilities or based on assumptions about family structure and sex roles that are outdated. As a consequence, many government programs and policies either actively hinder or hurt families, or are not as efficient and effective as they would be if they took families into account.[11]

Another problem shared by many government policies or programs is pitting one group against another through categorical programs (e.g., programs for children versus women versus the elderly). Another example is provided by those who argue for limiting the numbers of immigrants and refugees who enter the United States (in most cases to rejoin their families); they erroneously suggest that these newcomers threaten the jobs and income levels of American citizens.

The Plan of Pastoral Action for Family Ministry speaks to the relationship between public policy and family life:

> Because the family always exists in relation to the wider society, careful attention must be given toward the constructive influence of public policy as it relates to family life. Implicit government policy and explicit government planning and programs can contribute to the erosion of the health and vitality of the family. Examples of this process are urban and neighborhood revitalization developments which favor the wealthy rather than the displaced poor, the creation of suburban sprawl which is determined primarily by the priorities of big business and real estate developers, and the spread of giant agribusiness at the expense of

the small family farm.[12] Comprehensive decisions of a national or regional scope must take into account their impact on family life. Families, especially whose influence is lessened by poverty or social status, must be allowed their rightful input in those decisions which affect their daily lives. This delicate, yet decisive, relationship between society and the family demands careful study, and where destructive influences on the family are apparent, society ought to be challenged in support of the rights of families.[13]

This sentiment is reaffirmed in the bishops' pastoral letter on the economy, which states: "Economic and social policies as well as the organization of the work world should be continually evaluated in light of their impact on the strength and stability of family life."[14]

Presently, a number of public-policy issues on the horizon need to take the family into account. First is the issue of dependent care across the life cycle:

> Families and government will continue to share economic, health, and protective care of the chronically ill, the handicapped, and the elderly. What will be the proper balance of responsibility? Will this shift toward institutions as the traditional caretaker—the adult daughter or female relative—become less available as she enters the labor force? Or will the shift be toward the family as health-care costs soar? Moroney (1980:15) phrases the underlying theoretical question as "What is the most desirable, effective, and feasible division between the family and extra familial institutions in meeting the need of individuals, and in what way can these institutions relate to each other to maximize benefits?" The most perplexing problem this issue raises is how to structure the public and private payment mechanisms toward incentives for family and community-based care and support.[15]

The second issue is one that concerns values, explicit or implicit, in public policy:

> Values are deeply embedded in all policy discussions about families, although rarely made explicit. A family perspective will only be useful if the basic value assumptions and goals of policy are carefully explicated, the moral dilemmas are openly debated, and the questions of fact are separated from the questions of values (to the extent possible).[16]

The third issue has to do with power: where families have power and where they are powerless in dealing with daily life and with crises. Policymakers and church leaders need to know what realistically can be expected of families today by way of handling both crises and ordinary life. Such assessment is not easily come by, since the question has become politically charged.

---

[9] *The Changing Family*, 147-148.
[10] T. Ooms, "The Necessity of a Family Perspective" in *Journal of Family Issues* 5:2 (June 1984): 146.
[11] Ibid., 146.

[12] Editor's Note: cf. F. Meis, "The Impact of the Rural Economy on Farm Families," *Families, the Economy, and the Church.*
[13] *The Plan of Pastoral Action for Family Ministry: A Vision and a Strategy* (Washington, D.C.: USCC Office of Publishing and Promotion Services, 1978), 5-6.
[14] *Economic Justice for All*, 93.
[15] "The Necessity of a Family Perspective," *Journal of Family Issues*, 175-176.
[16] Ibid., 170.

There are some—heirs to a branch of social theory—who view the family as a patient in need, who maintain that families can do nothing well for themselves and need the direction of experts for survival. There are others—often advocates for cutting government services—who say that only culpable moral weakness prevents families from meeting all their own needs. Each of these viewpoints has vocal advocates. In order to have the information necessary to plan policies and programs, policymakers and social leaders need to avoid these polarized views in favor of an accurate assessment of the strengths and needs to be found in American families.

A fourth issue regards human service providers. Such professionals are, by and large, trained to work with individuals. However, they also need to be taught about family systems, diversity, and responsibilities so that they may be better able to put their skills and knowledge to use. In other words, in addition to the professional training that helps them to master their field, they also need to learn how to share their information, decision making, and power with client families.[17] As some leaders in professional education will admit, this aspect of professional education often receives little attention.

Family Impact Questions

To incorporate a family perspective that takes into account the necessary partnership between families and social institutions, leaders need to ask themselves questions similiar to the following about their specific policy, program, ministry, or service:

- In what concrete ways does it complicate or assist families in their difficult new responsibility of co-ordinating multiple services?
- Does it objectively state that families are equal partners in the service, or does it tend to marginalize or limit family responsibility?
- How does it seek to involve participating families in its planning, implementation, and evaluation?
- How does it concretely broaden the choices and options of participating families?
- In what specific ways does it attempt to get the information to families that they might need to fulfill their responsibilities?
- How does it promote the family as a mediating structure between its individual members and social institutions?

---

[17] Ibid., 171.

Family Impact Questions for Public Policy[18]

The family impact questions that follow should be asked by policymakers about the specific policy, program, or service:

- How does it protect the developmental, environmental, and political rights of families?
- Does it lessen earned household income? If so, how do the benefits of this action outweigh and justify the exaction from the family budget?
- How does it serve to reinforce the stability of the home and, particularly, the marital commitment that holds the home together?
- In what ways does it strengthen or erode the authority of the home and, specifically, the rights of parents in the education, nurturance, and supervision of their children?
- How does it protect the family from unwarranted intrusion and allow parents' choice?
- How does it enhance individual development of competence and self-realization and protect individual members of the family from abuse and severe neglect?
- In what concrete ways does it help the family perform its responsibilities and prevent government activities from substituting for that responsibility?
- How does it improve the capacity of families to master a broad range of developmental tasks and promote family strengths?
- How does it improve the liaison or linkage functions related to social resources and supports needed by families?
- Does it subject people to humiliating circumstances and suggest that they have an inferior status, thus devaluing and stigmatizing them and causing them to suffer a loss of self-esteem?
- Is it divisive, in that it gives unwarranted advantage to some; separates people for unwarranted reasons on the basis of age, sex, racial, and ethnic group membership; socioeconomic status; education level; and the like?
- Does it promote marriage and family enrichment groups and associations as partners in the common tasks of supporting and assisting families?
- What message, intended or otherwise, does the policy, program, or service send to the public concerning the status of the family?

---

[18] Cf. *A General Educational Guide to Family Impact Studies*; R. M. Moroney, *Families, Social Services and Social Policy: The Issue of Shared Responsibility* (Washington, D.C.: U.S. Government Printing Office, 1980); "Actualizing Family Rights"; and G. L. Bauer, ed., *The Nation's Families* (Washington, D.C.: U.S. Department of Education, 1986).

AFFIRMATION AND CHALLENGES

The committee hopes this manual affirms ministers in the Church—lay, religious, and ordained—who are implementing the vision of family life presented in *The Plan of Pastoral Action for Family Ministry, Familiaris Consortio,* and the *Charter of the Rights of the Family.* These ministers are making great efforts to support the unity, health, well-being, and stability of family life. They have made great strides in ministering to, with, for, and by families. The committee also affirms pastoral leaders in ministries not directly related to family life, but who have made a conscious effort to support married persons and families in their programs. The committee also affirms leaders in society (social institutions, government, and other religious groups) who are promoting the well-being and stability of family life.

Nevertheless, the need to continue such efforts in a more systematic way, by incorporating a family perspective in the Church's policies, programs, ministries, and services, is an urgent one. What remains are some fundamental needs that challenge the entire Church and each of our social institutions:

- Greater theological study of the church of the home and its implications for the parish community, as well as the issues of marriage, intimacy, and family life.

- Development of models of empowerment for families, which will help them integrate their four tasks as specified in *Familiaris Consortio.*
- Greater integration of the insights of the sciences of family relations and family systems into pastoral reflection and practice.
- A methodology for regularly gathering emerging data about family life, to serve as a basis for program revision.
- A systematic analysis of how cultural, economic, and political systems affect family life and values.
- Models of partnership between families and those institutions that share its responsibilities.
- Development and promotion, on behalf of families, of a shared agenda that promotes family rights with other social and ecclesial institutions.
- Implementation of ongoing evaluations, at each level of the Church, of its policies, programs, ministries, and services, to determine how they support or undermine family life.
- A detailed explication, by every ministry of the Church, of its inherent family component.
- A systematic revision of programs of ministry training and formation to incorporate the family dimension of the particular discipline.

The committee once again urges that the appropriate persons in national offices, in dioceses, and in parishes be convened to study and weigh the ideas contained in this manual and to judge the ramifications for ecclesial and social policies, programs, ministries, and services.

The committee urges interested persons to continue to deepen their understanding of the elements of a family perspective by undertaking a program of reading as outlined in the *Reading Guide* that follows in the next section. Further, resources focusing on how to implement a family perspective are described at the end of this manual.

A READING GUIDE FOR FURTHER STUDY OF A FAMILY PERSPECTIVE AND ITS ELEMENTS

This Reading Guide is intended to assist interested persons in deepening their understanding of a "family perspective" and its elements. It consists of a short *Reading List*, followed by a comprehensive listing of *References and Readings*.

A Reading List

The following list of readings is organized by subjects as they appear in this manual.

Social Change and the Family

Bane, M. J. *Here to Stay: American Families in the Twentieth Century*. New York: Basic Books, 1976.

Levitan, S. and R. Belous. *What's Happening to America's Families?* Baltimore: Johns Hopkins, 1981.

Masnick, G. and M. J. Bane. *The Nation's Families: 1960-1990*. Boston: Auburn House, 1980.

Preister, S. "Social Change and the Family: An Historical Perspective with Family Impact Assessment Principles for Catholic Charities." *Social Thought*. Summer 1982.

————. "Marriage, Divorce, and Remarriage in the United States, and Application to American Catholics." *Catholic Remarriage: Pastoral Issues and Preparation Models*. S. Preister and J. J. Young, eds. Mahwah, N.J.: Paulist Press, 1986.

Theology of Marriage and the Family, Family Ministry, Spirituality, Prayer

Durkin, M. *Feast of Love: Pope John Paul II on Human Intimacy*. Chicago: Loyola University Press, 1983.

Huck, G. *A Book of Family Prayer*. New York: Seabury Press, 1979.

John Paul II. *Familiaris Consortio* Apostolic Exhortation on the Family. Washington, D.C.: USCC Office of Publishing and Promotion Services, 1981.

Kasper, W. *Theology of Christian Marriage*. New York: Crossroad, 1981.

Lynch, T. and F. Mauro. "Young Adults and Their Family of Origin." *Young Adult Ministry Resources*. Washington D.C.: USCC Office of Publishing and Promotion Services. Forthcoming 1988.

National Association of Catholic Diocesan Family Life Ministers. *The Sacred in the Ordinary*. 1984.

National Conference of Catholic Bishops. *Human Life in Our Day*. Pastoral Letter of the U.S. Bishops. Washington, D.C.: USCC Office of Publishing and Promotion Services, 1968. Out of Print.

————, Committee on the Liturgy. *Book of Household Blessings and Prayers*. Washington, D.C.: USCC Office of Publishing and Promotion Services. Forthcoming 1988.

United States Catholic Conference. *The Plan of Pastoral Action for Family Ministry: A Vision and Strategy*. Washington, D.C.: USCC Office of Publishing and Promotion Services, 1978. Out of Print.

Second Vatican Council. "The Pastoral Constitution on the Church in the Modern World" (*Gaudium et Spes*). See *The Documents of Vatican II*. W. M. Abbott, SJ, ed. Piscataway, N.J.: Association Press/New Century Publishers, Inc., 1966.

Family Systems and Family of Origin

Friedman, E. *Generation to Generation: Family Process in Church and Synagogue*. New York: Guilford Press, 1985.

Galvin, K. M. and B. J. Brommel. *Family Communication: Cohesion and Change*. Second Edition. Glenview, Ill.: Scott, Foresman and Company, 1986.

Guernsey, D. *A New Design for Family Ministry*. Elgin, Ill.: David Cook Publisher Company, 1982.

Kantor, D. and W. Lehr. *Inside the Family: Toward a Theory of Family Process*. San Francisco: Jossey-Bass, 1975. Reprint E. New York: Harper Colophon Books/Harper & Row, 1976.

Minuchin, S. *Families and Family Therapy*. Cambridge: Harvard University Press, 1974.

Family Strengths and Family Health

Curran, D. *Traits of the Healthy Family*. Minneapolis: Winston Press, 1983.

Morgan, E. A. *Pioneer Research on Strong, Healthy Families*. Washington, D.C.: The Family Research Council, 1987.

Sacred Congregation for Catholic Education. *Educational Guidance in Human Love*. Washington, D.C.: USCC Office of Publishing and Promotion Services, 1983.

USCC Commission on Marriage and Family Life. *A Positive Vision for Family Life: A Resource Guide for Pope John Paul II's Apostolic Exhortation "Familiaris Consortio."* Washington, D.C.: USCC Office of Publishing and Promotion Services, 1985.

Family Life Cycle

Carter, E. A. and M. McGoldrick. *The Family Lifecycle*. New Jersey: Halsted, 1980.

Family Diversity, Culture, Economics, Heritages

Hoge, D. R. and K. W. Ferry. *Empirical Research on Interfaith Marriage in America*. Washington, D.C.: United States Catholic Conference, 1981.

Kluckhohn, F. "Variations in the Basic Values of Family Systems." *A Modern Introduction to the Family*. E. Bell and S. Vogel, eds. New York: Basic Books, 1968.

Mindel, C. H. and R. Heberstein. *Ethnic Families in America*. New York: Elsevier Press.

Schervish, P. "Family Life and the Economy: Graver Responsibilities and Scarcer Resources." *Families, the Economy, and the Church: A Book of Readings and Discussion Guide*. F. Brigham, Jr., and S. Preister, eds. Washington, D.C.: USCC Office of Publishing and Promotion Services, 1987.

USCC Commission on Marriage and Family Life. *Families: Black and Catholic, Catholic and Black*. Sr. T. Bowman, FSPA, Ph.D., ed. Washington, D.C.: USCC Office of Publishing and Promotion Services, 1985.

Yankelovich, D. *New Rules: Searching for Self-Fulfillment in a World Turned Upside Down*. New York: Random House, 1981.

Family History

Aries, P. *Centuries of Childhood*. New York: Vintage Books/Random House, 1982.

Becker, G. *A Treatise on the Family*. Cambridge, Mass.: Harvard University Press, 1981.

Bellah, R. N., R. Madsen, W. M. Sullivan, A. Swidler and S. M. Tipton. *Habits of the Heart: Individualism and Commitment in American Life*. Berkeley: University of California Press, 1985.

Berger, B. and P. Berger. *The War Over the Family*. New York: Anchor/Doubleday, 1983.

Hareven, T. Testimony before the U.S. House of Representatives' Select Committee on Children, Youth, and Families. Washington, D.C.: Government Printing Office, February 25, 1986. Pp. 28-40.

Lasch, C. *Haven in a Heartless World: The Family Beseiged*. New York: Basic Books, 1977.

Shorter, E. *The Making of the Modern Family*. New York: Basic Books, 1975.

Families and Social Institutions

Berger, P. L. and R. J. Neuhaus. *To Empower People: The Role of Mediating Structures in Public Policy*. Washington, D.C.: American Enterprise Institute for Public Policy Research, 1977.

Farkis, S. *Taking a Family Perspective: A Principal's Guide for Working with Families of Handicapped Children*. Washington, D.C.: The Family Impact Seminar, The National Center for Family Studies at The Catholic University of America, 1981.

—————. *Hospitalized Children: The Family's Role in Their Care and Treatment*. Washington, D.C.: The Family Impact Seminar, The National Center for Family Studies at The Catholic University of America, 1984.

Hayes, C., T. Ooms, D. Guttman and P. Mahon-Stetson. *The Euro-American Elderly in the United States: A Manual for Service Providers and Ethnic Leaders*. Washington, D.C.: Center for the Study of Pre-Retirement and Aging at The Catholic University of America, 1986.

Henderson, A. T., C. L. Marburger and T. Ooms. *Beyond the Bake Sale: An Educator's Guide to Working with Parents*. Columbia, Md.: National Committee for Citizens in Education, 1986.

Kahn, A. and S. Kamerman. *Helping America's Families*. Philadelphia: Temple University Press, 1982.

Kinch, R., ed. *Strengthening Families through Informal Support Systems: A Wingspread Report*. Racine, Wis.: The Johnson Foundation, 1979.

Statuto, C., et al. *Families in the 80s: Implications for Employers and Human Services*. Washington, D.C.: The Family Impact Seminar, The National Center for Family Studies at The Catholic University of America, 1984.

Social Policy and the Family, and Family Impact Studies

Kamerman, S. and A. Kahn. *Family Policy: Government and Families in Fourteen Countries*. New York: Columbia University Press, 1978.

Moynihan, D. P. *Family and Nation*. New York: Harcourt Brace Jovanovich, 1986.

National Conference of Catholic Bishops. *The Pastoral Plan for Pro-Life Activities: A Reaffirmation*. Washington, D.C.: USCC Office of Publishing and Promotion Services, 1985.

—————. *Economic Justice for All: Pastoral Letter on Catholic Social Teaching and the U.S. Economy*. Washington, D.C.: USCC Office of Publishing and Promotion Services, 1986.

Ooms, T. "The Necessity of a Family Perspective." Special Report on Family Policy. *Journal of Family Issues* 5:2 (June 1984): 160-181.

—————. *A General Educational Guide to Family Impact Studies*. Washington, D.C.: The Family Impact Seminar, The National Center for Family Studies at The Catholic University of America, January 1985.

Preister, S., et al., *Family Criteria in Policymaking and Program Analysis: A Report of the Family Criteria Task*

Force to the U.S. House of Representatives' Select Committee on Children, Youth, and Families. Washington, D.C.: American Association for Marriage and Family Therapy, January 1, 1988.

Vatican. *Charter of the Rights of the Family.* Washington, D.C.: USCC Office of Publishing and Promotion Services, 1983.

References and Readings

Abbott, P. *The Family on Trial: Special Relationships in Modern Political Thought.* University Park: Pennsylvania State University, 1981.

Abbott, W. M., ed. *The Documents of Vatican II.* See "The Pastoral Constitution on the Church in the Modern World" (*Gaudium et Spes*). See "The Declaration on Christian Education" (*Gravissimum Educationis*). Piscataway, N.J.: Association Press/New Century Publishers, Inc., 1966.

Alessio, L. and H. Munoz. *Marriage and the Family.* New York: Society of St. Paul, 1982.

Alwin, D. F. "Trends in Parental Socialization Values: Detroit, 1958 to 1983." *American Journal of Sociology* 90:3 (1984): 359-370.

Anderson and Gribben, eds. *The Family in the Modern World.* Washington, D.C.: American Family Institute, 1982.

Aries, P. *Centuries of Childhood.* New York: Vintage Books/Random House, 1962.

Bane, M. J. *Here to Stay: American Families in the Twentieth Century.* New York: Basic Books, 1976.

Bauer, G. L., ed. *The Nation's Families.* A Report of President Reagan's Working Group on the Family. Washington, D.C.: U.S. Department of Education, 1986. Pp. 63-64.

Beavers, W. R. and M. N. Voeller. "Family Models: Comparing and Contrasting the Olson Circumplex Model with the Beavers System Model." *Family Process* 22 (March 1983): 85-98.

Becker, G. *A Treatise on the Family.* Cambridge, Mass.: Harvard University Press, 1981.

Bellah, R. N., R. Madsen, W. M. Sullivan, A. Swidler and S. M. Tipton. *Habits of the Heart: Individualism and Commitment in American Life.* Berkeley: University of California Press, 1985.

Berger, B. and P. Berger. *The War Over the Family.* New York: Anchor/Doubleday, 1983.

Berger, P. L. and R. J. Neuhaus. *To Empower People: The Role of Mediating Structures in Public Policy.* Washington, D.C.: American Enterprise Institute for Public Policy Research, 1977.

Blake, J. "Catholicism and Fertility: On Attitudes of Young Americans." *Population and Development Review* (June 1984).

Bockle, F., ed. *The Future of Marriage as an Institution.* New York: Herder and Herder, 1970.

Bohen, H. H. and A. Viveros-Long. *Balancing Jobs and Family Life: Do Flexible Work Schedules Help?* Philadelphia: Temple University Press, 1981.

Boland, T. Unpublished Personal Notes. Louisville, Ky.: Family Life Office, 1986.

Bowen, M. "Toward a Differentiation of a Self in One's Own Family." *Family Therapy in Clinical Practice,* M. Bowen, ed. New York: Jason Aronson, 1978. Pp. 467-528.

Bronfenbrenner, U. and H. Weiss. "Beyond Policies without People: An Ecological Perspective on Child and Family Policy." *Children, Families, and Government: Perspectives on American Social Policy.* E. Zigler, S. Kagan and E. Klugman, eds. Cambridge, Mass.: Cambridge University Press, 1983.

Burr, W. R. and G. K. Leigh. "Famology: A New Discipline." *Journal of Marriage and the Family* 45 (August 1983): 467-480.

Burtchaell, J. T., ed. *Marriage Among Christians.* Notre Dame: Ave Maria Press, 1977.

————. *For Better, For Worse.* New York: Paulist Press, 1985.

Campolo, T. "The Death of Traditional Parenthood." *Youthworker* (Spring 1985): 43.

Canon Law Society of America, trans. *Code of Canon Law, Latin-English Edition.* Washington, D.C.: Canon Law Society of America, 1983.

Caplow, T. *Middletown Families: Fifty Years of Change and Continuity.* Minneapolis: University of Minnesota Press, 1982.

Carnes. P. *Family Development I: Understanding Us.* Minneapolis: Interpersonal Communication Programs, Inc., 1981.

Carter, E. A. and M. McGoldrick. *The Family Lifecycle.* New Jersey: Halsted, 1980.

Cherlin, A. Testimony Presented to the U.S. House of Representatives' Select Committee on Children, Youth, and Families. Washington, D.C.: Government Printing Office, 1986. Pp. 40-44.

Clinebell, H. J. and C. H. Clinebell. *The Intimate Marriage.* New York: Harper & Row, 1970.

Coalition of Family Organizations. *COFO Memo.* Quarterly Newsletter. Washington, D.C.: American Association for Marriage and Family Therapy (December 1986): 1ff.

Collins, A. H. and D. L. Pancoast. *Natural Helping Networks: A Strategy for Prevention.* Washington, D.C.: National Association of Social Workers, 1978.

Connery, J. "The Role of Love in Marriage: An Historical Review." *Communio* (Fall 1984).

Constantine, L. L. "Dysfunction and Failure in Open Family Systems I: Application of a Unified Theory." *Journal of Marriage and the Family* 45 (November 1983): 725-738.

Curran, D. *Traits of the Healthy Family.* Minneapolis: Winston Press, 1983.

————. *Stress and the Healthy Family.* New York: Harper and Row, 1985.

D'Antonio, W. and J. Aldous, eds. *Families and Religions.* Beverly Hills: Sage Publications, 1983.

Dennehy, R. *Christian Married Love.* San Francisco: Ignatius Press, 1981.

Derrick, C. *Sex and Sacredness.* San Francisco: Ignatius Press, 1982.

Dolan, J. P. and D. C. Leege. *A Profile of American Catholic Parishes and Parishioners: 1820s to the 1980s.* Report No. 2. D. C. Leege and J. Gremillion, eds. Notre Dame, Ind.: Notre Dame Study of Catholic Parish Life, University of Notre Dame, February 1985.

Doyle, P., ed. *Marriage Studies III.* Washington, D.C.: Canon Law Society of America, 1985.

Durkin, M. *Feast of Love: Pope John Paul II on Human Intimacy.* Chicago: Loyola University Press, 1983.

Dyck, A. "The Moral Bonds of the Family." *Linacre Quarterly* (February 1981).

Family Impact Seminar. *Toward an Inventory of Federal Programs with Direct Impact on Families.* Staff Report. Washington, D.C.: The Family Impact Seminar, The National Center for Family Studies at The Catholic University of America, 1978.

————. *Interim Report.* Washington, D.C.: The Family Impact Seminar, 1978.

Farkis, S. *Taking a Family Perspective: A Principal's Guide for Working with Families of Handicapped Children.* Washington, D.C.: The Family Impact Seminar, 1981.

————. *Hospitalized Children: The Family's Role in Their Care and Treatment.* Washington, D.C.: The Family Impact Seminar, 1984.

Finley, M. "Family Orphaned by the Church." *National Catholic Reporter* (February 28, 1986): 11-12.

———— and K. Finley. "The Sacredness of the Ordinary." *Family Spirituality: The Sacred in the Ordinary.* The National Association of Catholic Diocesan Family Life Ministers, 1984.

Fox, G. L., ed. *The Childbearing Decision.* Beverly Hills: Sage Publications, 1982.

Fraiberg, S. *Every Child's Birthright: In Defense of Mothering.* New York: Basic Books, 1977.

Friedman, E. *Generation to Generation: Family Process in Church and Synagogue.* New York: Guilford Press, 1985.

Furstenberg, F. F. and C. W. Nord. "Parenting Apart: Patterns of Childrearing after Marital Disruption." *Journal of Marriage and the Family* 47:4 (November 1985): 893-904

Gallagher, C., et al. *Embodied in Love: Sacramental Spirituality and Sexual Intimacy.* New York: Crossroad, 1983.

Gallup, G. *American Families—1980.* Princeton, N.J.: The Gallup Organization, 1980.

————. "Attitudes of the U.S. Public toward Marriage and the Family." Testimony before U.S. Senate Subcommittee on Family and Human Services Hearing, "Broken Families: Overview and Effects on Children," March 22, 1983.

Galvin, K. M. and B. J. Brommel. *Family Communication: Cohesion and Change.* Second Edition. Glenview, Ill.: Scott, Foresman and Co., 1986.

Garland, Sr. B. "The Church as Workplace and Its Impact on Family Life." *Families, the Economy, and the Church: A Book of Readings and Discussion Guide.* F. Brigham, Jr., and S. Preister, eds. Washington, D.C.: USCC Office of Publishing and Promotion Services, 1987.

Glazer, N. and D. P. Moynihan. *Beyond the Melting Pot.* Cambridge, Mass.: MIT Press, 1965.

Greeley, A., ed. *The Family in Crisis or in Transition.* Concilium Series, vol. 121. New York: Seabury, 1979.

————. *The Young Catholic Family: Religious Images and Marital Fulfillment.* Chicago: The Thomas More Press, 1980.

————. "Study of American Catholics Is Misleading." *The New York Times.* Letter to the Editor. March 21, 1985.

Greenblatt, C. S. "The Salience of Sexuality in the Early Years of Marriage." *Journal of Marriage and the Family* (May 1983).

Grelot, P. *Man and Wife in Scripture.* New York: Herder and Herder, 1964.

Guarino, C. "Canonical and Theological Perspectives on Marriage, Divorce, and Remarriage." *Catholic Remarriage: Pastoral Issues and Preparation Models.* S. Preister and J. J. Young, eds. Mahwah, N.J.: Paulist Press, 1986.

Guernsey, D. *A New Design For Family Ministry.* Elgin, Ill.: David Cook Publishers Co, 1982.

Haraven, T. "Themes in the Historical Development of the Family." *The Family: Review of Child Development Research.* Vol 7. Parke, ed. Chicago: University of Chicago Press, 1984. Pp. 137-178.

————. Testimony before the U.S. House of Representatives' Select Committee on Children, Youth, and Families. Washington, D.C.: Government Printing Office, February 25, l986. Pp. 28-40.

Harblin, T. D. "Actualizing Family Rights: Christian Participation in the Development of National and International Society." *The Changing Family: Reflections on Familiaris Consortio.* S. L. Saxton, P. Voydanoff and A. A. Zukowski, eds. Chicago: Loyola University Press, 1984.

Harrington, W. *The Promise to Love.* New York: Alba House, 1968.

Hauerwas, S. *A Community of Character.* Notre Dame: University of Notre Dame Press, 1981.

Hayes, C. *Women in the Middle.* Gainesville, Fla.: Triad Publications, 1986.

————, T. Ooms, D. Guttman and P. Mahon-Stetson. *The Euro-American Elderly in the United States: A Manual for Service Providers and Ethnic Leaders.* Washington, D.C.: Center for the Study of Pre-Retirement and Aging at The Catholic University of America, 1986.

Henderson, A. T., C. L. Marburger and T. Ooms. *Beyond the Bake Sale: An Educator's Guide to Working with Parents.* Columbia, Md.: National Committee for Citizens in Education, 1986.

Hetherington, E. "Children of Divorce." *Parent-Child Interaction.* R. Henderson, ed. New York: Academic Press, 1981.

Hill, R. *The Strengths of Black Families.* New York: Emerson Hall Publishers, 1971.

Hoge, D. R. and K. Ferry. *Empirical Research on Inter-faith Marriage in America*. Washington, D.C.: United States Catholic Conference, 1981.

Holland, J. "Family, Work, and Culture—Strategic Themes in the Crisis of Modernity." Washington, D.C.: The Center of Concern, 1986.

Hubbard, H. "Developing a Family Perspective in Society and in the Church." *Origins* 15:9 (1985): 313, 315-321.

Hubbell, R. *Foster Care and Families: Conflicting Values and Policies*. Philadelphia: Temple University Press, 1981.

Huck, G. *A Book of Family Prayer*. New York: Seabury Press, 1979.

Iannone, M. "The Dearest Freshness: Images of Family Life from a Faith Perspective." *Families and Television: A Book of Readings*. F. Brigham, Jr., and S. Preister, eds. Washington, D.C.: The National Center for Family Studies at The Catholic University of America, 1987.

Jansen, G. "The Sacrament of Matrimony." *The Sacramental We*. Milwaukee: Bruce and Company, 1968.

John Paul II. *Familiaris Consortio*. Papal Exhortation on the Family. Washington, D.C.: USCC Office of Publishing and Promotion Services, 1981.

————. *Original Unity of Man and Woman*. 1979-1980 Audience Talks. Boston: Daughters of St. Paul, 1981.

————. *Blessed Are the Pure of Heart*. 1980-1981 Audience Talks. Boston: Daughters of St. Paul, 1983.

————. *Reflections on Humanae Vitae: Conjugal Morality and Spirituality*. Summer 1984 Audience Talks. Boston: Daughters of St. Paul, 1984.

————. "Homily" delivered at Perth, Australia, November 30, 1986. Washington, D.C., 1986.

Kahn, A. and S. Kamerman. *Family Policy: Government and Families in Fourteen Countries*. New York: Columbia University Press, 1978.

————. *Helping America's Families*. Philadelphia: Temple University Press, 1982.

Kamerman, S. and C. Hayes, eds. *Families That Work*. Washington, D.C.: National Academy Press, 1982.

Kantor, D. and W. Lehr. *Inside the Family: Toward a Theory of Family Process*. San Francisco: Jossey-Bass, 1975. Reprint Edition, New York: Harper Colophon Books/Harper & Row, 1976.

Kasper, W. *Theology of Christian Marriage*. New York: Crossroads, 1981.

Keniston, K. *All Our Children: The American Family Under Pressure*. New York: Harcourt Brace Jovanovich, 1977.

Kilmartin, E. J. "When Is Marriage a Sacrament?" *Theological Studies* (June 1973): 275-286.

Kinch, R., ed. *Strengthening Families through Informal Support Systems: A Wingspread Report*. Racine, Wis.: The Johnson Foundation, 1979.

King, Jr., M. L. "Address" at Abbot House, Westchester County, New York. October 1965. Quoted in D. P. Moynihan's *Family and Nation*. New York: Harcourt Brace Jovanovich, 1986.

Kippley, J. *Birth Control and the Marriage Covenant*. Collegeville, Minn.: The Liturgical Press, 1981.

Klaus, H., et al. "Valuing the Procreative Capacity: A New Approach to Teens." *International Review of Natural Family Planning* (Fall 1984).

Kluckhohn, F. "Variations in the Basic Values of Family Systems." *A Modern Introduction to the Family*. E. Bell and S. Vogel, eds. New York: Basic Books, 1968.

Knaub, P., S. Hanna and N. Stinnett. "Strengths of Remarried Families." *Journal of Divorce* 7 (Fall 1984): 41-55.

Kramer, R. *In Defense of the Family: Raising Children in America Today*. New York: Basic Books, 1983.

LaCerte, H. "Theological Reflection on Marriage as a Humanizing Experience in a Dehumanizing World." *Marriage Studies II*. T. Doyle, ed. Washington, D.C.: Canon Law Society of America, 1982.

Lasch, C. *Haven in a Heartless World: The Family Besieged*. New York: Basic Books, 1977.

Laucks, E. *The Meaning of Children*. Boulder, Colo.: Westview, 1981.

Lawler, R., et al. *Catholic Sexual Ethics*. Huntington, Ind.: Our Sunday Visitor Press, 1985.

Lederer, W. J. and D. D. Jackson. *The Mirages of Marriage*. New York: W. W. Norton and Company, 1968.

Levitan, S. and R. Belous. *What's Happening to America's Families?* Baltimore: Johns Hopkins, 1981.

Levy, F. and R. Michel. *Urban Institute Report*. Washington, D.C., 1985.

Lewis, J. D. and S. Preister. "The Divorce and Remarriage Experiences in the U.S.: Emotional and Social Issues." *Catholic Remarriage: Pastoral Issues and Preparation Models*. S. Preister and J. J. Young, eds. Mahwah, N.J.: Paulist Press, 1986.

Lewis, J. M. *How's Your Family? A Guide to Identifying Your Family's Strengths and Weaknesses*. New York: Brunner/Mazel, 1979.

————, W. B. Beavers, J. Gossett and V. A. Phillips. *No Single Thread: Psychological Health in Family Systems*. New York: Brunner/Mazel, 1976.

Lynch, T. "A Family Sensitivity in Adult Religious Education." *1987 Christian Adulthood*. N. Parent, ed. Washington, D.C.: USCC Office of Publishing and Promotion Services, 1987.

————. "What Is the Method of Today's Families Madness?" *Momentum* (September 1987). Washington, D.C.: National Catholic Education Association.

———— and F. Mauro. "Young Adults and Their Family of Origin." *Young Adult Ministry Resources*. Washington, D.C.: USCC Office of Publishing and Promotion Services. Forthcoming 1988.

Mace, D. R., ed. *Prevention in Family Services: Approaches to Family Wellness*. Beverly Hills: Sage Publications, 1983.

Malone, R. and J. Connery, eds. *Contemporary Perspectives on Christian Marriage*. Chicago: Loyola University Press, 1984.

Manser, E. *Family Advocacy: A Manual for Action*. Milwaukee: Family Service America, 1973.

Martelet, G. "The Church as Sacrament." *Theology Digest* (Spring 1974): 62-67.

Martin, M. C. "Fertility Awareness and Natural Family Planning." *Respect Life Manual*. Washington, D.C.: United States Catholic Conference, 1981-1982.

Martin, T. M. *Christian Family Values*. New York: Paulist Press, 1984.

Masnick, G. and M. J. Bane. *The Nation's Families: 1960-1990*. Cambridge, Mass.: Joint Center for Urban Studies at Massachusetts Institute of Technology and Harvard University, 1980.

May, W. *Sex, Marriage and Chastity*. Chicago: Franciscan Herald Press, 1981.

————. "Role of the Christian Family, Articles 49-58." *Pope John Paul II and the Family*. Chicago: Franciscan Herald Press, 1983.

————. *Sex and the Sanctity of Life*. Front Royal, Va.: Christendom Publications, 1984.

McAdoo, H. P. "Afro-American Families: An Element of Actualization." *Families: Black and Catholic, Catholic and Black*. Sr. T. Bowman, FSPA, Ph.D., ed. Washington, D.C.: USCC Office of Publishing and Promotion Services, 1985.

McCarthy, D. "Biblical Personalism and Natural Family Planning." *Pastoral Life* (May 1973).

————. *Moral Theology Today: Certitudes and Doubts*. St. Louis: Pope John XXIII Medical Moral Center, 1983.

———— and E. Bayer. *Handbook on Critical Moral Issues*. St. Louis: Pope John XXIII Medical Moral Center, 1983.

McCubbin, H. I. "Family Adaptation to Crises." *Family Stress, Coping and Social Support*. H. I. McCubbin, A. E. Cauble and J. M. Patterson, eds. Springfield, Ill.: Charles C. Thomas, 1982.

————. "The Family Stress Process: The Double ABC-X Model of Adjustment and Adaptation." *Social Stress and the Family: Advances and Developments in Family Stress Theory and Research*. H. I. McCubbin, M. B. Sussman and J.M. Patterson, eds. *Marriage and Family Review* 5:1,2. New York: Haworth, 1983.

———— and J. M. Patterson. "Broadening the Scope of Family Strengths: An Emphasis on Family Coping and Social Support." *Family Strengths 3: Roots of Well-Being*. N. Stinnett, et al., eds. Lincoln: University of Nebraska Press, 1981. Pp. 177-194.

McGoldrick, M., et al., eds. *Ethnicity and Family Therapy*. New York: Guilford Press, 1982.

McHugh, J., ed. *Marriage in the Light of Vatican II*. Washington, D.C.: Family Life Bureau, U.S. Catholic Conference, 1968.

————. "The Synod, the Pope, and Respect for Life." *Respect Life Manual*. Washington, D.C.: U.S. Catholic Conference, 1981-1982.

————. *A Theological Perspective on Natural Family Planning*. Washington, D.C.: Diocesan Development Program for NFP, 1983.

————. "The Person, the Family and Fundamental Choices." *Respect Life Manual*. Washington, D.C.: United States Catholic Conference, 1983-1984.

Meis, F. "The Impact of the Rural Economy on Farm Families." *Families, the Economy, and the Church: A Book of Readings and Discussion Guide*. F. Brigham, Jr., and S. Preister, eds. Washington, D.C.: USCC Office of Publishing and Promotion Services, 1987.

Mindel, C. H. and R. Heberstein. *Ethnic Families in America*. New York: Elsevier Press.

Minuchin, S. *Families and Family Therapy*. Cambridge, Mass.: Harvard University Press, 1974.

Morgan, E. A. *Pioneer Research on Strong, Healthy Families*. Washington, D.C.: The Family Research Council, 1987.

Moroney, R. M. *Families, Social Services and Social Policy: The Issue of Shared Responsibility*. Washington, D.C.: U.S. Government Printing Office, 1980. DHHS Publication no. 80-846.

Mosher, W. D. and G. E. Hendershot. "Religion and Fertility Reexamined." Paper Presented at the Annual Meeting of the Population Association of America. Pittsburgh, 1983.

Moynihan, D. P. *Family and Nation*. New York: Harcourt Brace Jovanovich, 1986.

Murray, C. *Losing Ground: American Social Policy*. New York: Basic Books, 1984.

National Association of Catholic Diocesan Family Life Ministers. *Family Spirituality: The Sacred in the Ordinary*. 1984.

National Catholic Educational Association. *That They May Know You*. Washington, D.C., 1982.

————. *The Catholic High School: A National Portrait*. Washington, D.C., 1984.

National Center for Family Studies at The Catholic University of America. "Family and Parish: Historical Tension?" *American Catholic Family* 1:2 (September 1982): 1, 10-12.

National Conference of Catholic Bishops. *Human Life in Our Day*. Pastoral Letter. Washington, D.C.: USCC Office of Publishing and Promotion Services, 1968. Out of Print.

————. *The Plan of Pastoral Action for Family Ministry: A Vision and Strategy*. Washington, D.C.: USCC Office of Publishing and Promotion Services, 1978.

————. *The Hispanic Presence: Challenge and Commitment*. Pastoral Letter on Hispanic Ministry. Washington, D.C.: USCC Office of Publishing and Promotion Services, 1983.

————. *Economic Justice for All: Pastoral Letter on Catholic Social Teaching and the U.S. Economy*. Washington, D.C.: Office of Publishing and Promotion Services, 1986.

————. *Pastoral Plan for Pro-Life Activities: A Reaffirmation*. Washington, D.C.: USCC Office of Publishing and Promotion Services, 1986.

————, Ad Hoc Committee on Marriage and Family Life. *Families, the Economy, and the Church: A Book of Readings and Discussion Guide*. F. Brigham, Jr., and S. Preister, eds. Washington, D.C.: USCC Office of Publishing and Promotion Services, 1987.

————, Committee on the Liturgy. *Book of Household Blessings and Prayers*. Washington, D.C.: USCC Office of Publishing and Promotion Services. Forthcoming 1988.

National Federation for Catholic Youth Ministry, in colaboration with National Catholic Educational Association; National Conference of Diocesan Directors of Religious Education; and Representative for Youth Ministry, United States Catholic Conference. *The Challenge of Adolescent Catechesis: Maturing in Faith.* Washington, D.C., 1986.

Noonan, J. "The Family and the Supreme Court." John XXIII Lecture. *The Catholic University of America Law Review* (Winter 1973).

Olson, D. H. and H. I. McCubbin, et al. *Families: What Makes Them Work.* Beverly Hills: Sage Publications, 1983.

————, D. H. Sprenkle and C. S. Russell. "Circumplex Model of Marital and Family Systems I: Cohesion and Adaptability Dimensions, Family Types, and Clinical Applications." *Family Process* 18 (1979): 3-28.

Ooms, T. "The Necessity of a Family Perspective." *Journal of Family Issues* 5:2 (June 1984): 160-181.

————. *A General Educational Guide to Family Impact Studies.* Washington, D.C.: The Family Impact Seminar, The National Center for Family Studies at The Catholic University of America, January 1985.

———— and S. Hanson. "The Economics of Two Earner Families: The Costs and Benefits of Maternal Employment." Commissioned by the Joint Economic Committee, U.S. Congress. Washington, D.C., 1987.

———— and A. S. Johnson III. *Taking Families Seriously: A Challenge for Social Policy.* Monograph Commissioned by the Project for the Federal Social Role. Washington, D.C., 1987.

———— and J. Smollar. *Young Unwed Fathers: Research Review and Policy Dilemmas and Options.* Report of a Project Performed for the Office of the Assistant Secretary for Planning and Evaluation, U.S. Department of Health and Human Services. Washington, D.C., 1987.

O'Rourke, D., A. D. Thompson, S. Preister, J. D. Lewis and M. K. Feldman. *Preparing for Marriage: A Study of Marriage Preparations in American Catholic Dioceses.* St. Meinrad, Ind.: Abbey Press, 1983.

Otto, H. A. "What Is a Strong Family?" *Marriage and Family Living* (February 1962): 77-80.

Palmer, P. F. "Rethinking the Marriage Bond." *America* (January 17, 1970): 39-42.

————. "Christian Marriage: Contract or Covenant?" *Theological Studies* (Spring 1972): 617-665.

————. "Needed: A Theology of Marriage." *Communio* (Fall 1974): 243-260.

Parrella, F. "Towards a Spirituality of the Family." *Communio* (Summer 1982).

Paul VI. *On the Regulation of Birth (Humanae Vitae).* Papal Encyclical. Washington, D.C.: USCC Office of Publishing and Promotion Services, 1968.

————, John Paul I and John Paul II. *The Family: Center of Life and Love.* Papal Addresses, 1972-1981. Boston: Daughters of St. Paul, 1981.

Peal, E. "'Normal' Sex Roles: An Historical Analysis." *Family Process* (September 1975).

Pope John XXIII Center. *The Family Today and Tomorrow.* Braintree, Mass.: Pope John XXIII Center, 1985.

Preston, S. "Children and the Elderly in the United States." *Scientific American* (December 1984).

Preister, S. "Social Change and the Family: An Historical Perspective with Family Impact Assessment Principles for Catholic Charities." *Social Thought* (Summer 1982).

————. "Contemporary American Families: Facts and Fables." Presentation to the 82nd Annual Convention of The National Catholic Educational Association (April 11, 1985). Washington, D.C.: The National Center for Family Studies at The Catholic University of America, 1985.

———— and Young, J. J., eds. *Catholic Remarriage: Pastoral Issues and Preparation Models.* Mahwah: N.J.: Paulist Press, 1986.

————, et al. *Family Criteria in Policymaking and Program Analysis: A Report of the Family Criteria Task Force to the U.S. House of Representatives' Select Committee on Children, Youth, and Families.* Washington, D.C.: American Association for Marriage and Family Therapy, January 1, 1988.

Quay, P. M. *The Christian Meaning of Human Sexuality.* Evanston, Ill.: Credo House, 1985.

Quinn, J. "Marriage, Covenant and Charism." *America* (September 27, 1980).

Rahner, K. *Foundations of Christian Faith:* 421.

————. "Marriage as a Sacrament." *Theological Investigations.* New York: Herder and Herder, 1973.

————. *The Church and the Sacraments.* New York: Herder and Herder, 1983. Pp. 11-19; 107-113.

Ramsey, P. *Fabricated Man.* New Haven: Yale Univerity Press, 1970.

Rekers, G., ed. *Family Building: Six Qualities of a Strong Family.* Ventura, Calif.: Regal Books, 1985.

Rich, S. "Hyping the Family's Decline." The *Washington Post* (July 26, 1987): B-5.

Rossi, A. "A Biosocial Perspective on Parenting." *Daedalus* (Spring 1977).

Rousseau, M. and C. Gallagher. *Sex is Holy.* Amity, N.Y.: Amity House, 1986.

Rueveni, U. *Networking Families in Crisis.* New York: Human Sciences Press, 1978.

Sawin, M. M. *Family Enrichment with Family Clusters.* Paramus, N.J.: Newman Press, 1970.

Saxon, S. L., P. Voydanoff and A. A. Zukowski, eds. *The Changing Family: Reflections on "Familiaris Consortio".* Chicago: Loyola University Press, 1984.

Schervish, P. "Family Life and the Economy: Graver Responsibilities and Scarcer Resources." *Families, the Economy, and the Church: A Book of Readings and Discussion Guide.* F. Brigham, Jr., and S. Preister, eds. Washington, D.C.: USCC Office of Publishing and Promotion Services, 1987.

Schillebeeckx, E. *Marriage: Human Reality and Saving Mystery.* New York: Sheed and Ward, 1965.

Sheehan, P. "Do Catholics Still Honor Traditional Values?" *Our Sunday Visitor.*

Shorter, E. *The Making of the Modern Family.* New York: Basic Books, 1975.

Statuto, C., et al. *Families in the 80s: Implications for Employers and Human Services.* Washington, D.C.: The Family Impact Seminar, The National Center for Family Studies at The Catholic University of America, 1984.

Stinnett, N. "In Search of Strong Families." *Building Family Strengths: Blueprints for Action.* N. Stinnett, B. Chesser and J. DeFrain, eds. Lincoln: University of Nebraska Press, 1979. Pp. 23-30.

————. "Strong Families: A Portrait." *Prevention in Family Services: Approaches to Family Wellness.* D. R. Mace, ed. Beverly Hills: Sage Publications, 1983. Pp. 27-38.

———— and K. H. Sauer. "Relationship Characteristics of Strong Families." *Family Perspective* 11 (1977): 3-11.

————, G. Sangers and J. DeFrain. "Strong Families: A National Study." *Family Strengths 3: Roots of Family Well-Being.* N. Stinnett, et al., eds. Lincoln: University of Nebraska Press, 1981. Pp. 33-41.

Synod of Bishops (1980). *The Role of the Christian Family in the Modern World.* Study Guide. Washington, D.C.: USCC Office of Publishing and Promotion Services, 1980.

Thomas, D. *Family Ministry.* St. Meinrad, Ind.: Abbey Press, 1978.

————. *God, Religion, and the Family.* St. Meinrad, Ind.: Abbey Press, 1978.

————. *Marital Spirituality.* St. Meinrad, Ind.: Abbey Press, 1978.

Thomas, J. L. "The Family in a Pluralistic Society." *Respect Life Manual.* Washington, D.C.: United States Catholic Conference, 1978-1979.

Thornton, A. "Family and Religion in a Changing World." Paper Presented to the Conference on Religion and the Family. Provo, Utah: Brigham Young University, March 7-8, 1984.

————. "Changing Attitudes toward Separation and Divorce: Causes and Consequences." *American Journal of Sociology* (1985).

Toffler, A. *The Third Wave.* New York: Morrow, 1980.

Toman, W. *Family Constellation.* New York: Springer Publishing Company, 1976.

Tomko, J. "Some Aspects of the Theology of Marriage Based on the Teaching of St. Paul." *The Laity Today* 17-18 (1974).

United States Catholic Conference. *Sharing the Light of Faith: National Catechetical Directory for Catholics of the United States.* Washington, D.C.: USCC Office of Publishing and Promotion Services, 1979.

————, in cooperation with Center for the Study of Youth Development at The Catholic University of America. *A National Inventory of Parish Catechetical Programs.* Washington, D.C.: USCC Office of Publishing and Promotion Services, 1978. Out of Print.

————, Commission on Marriage and Family Life. *Families: Black and Catholic, Catholic and Black.* Sr. T. Bowman, FSPA, Ph.D., ed. Washington, D.C.: USCC Office of Publishing and Promotion Services, 1985.

————. *A Positive Vision for Family Life: A Resource Guide for Pope John Paul II's Apostolic Exhortation "Familiaris Consortio".* Washington, D.C.: USCC Office of Publishing and Promotion Services, 1985.

U.S. House of Representatives. *The Diversity and Strength of American Families.* February 25, 1986, Hearing before the Select Committee on Children, Youth, and Families. Washington, D.C.: U.S. Government Printing Office, 1986. Publication No. 60-802-0.

Van Der Poel, C. *God's Love in Human Language.* Pittsburgh: Duquesne University Press, 1969.

Varenne, H. "The Family: A Modern Anthropological Perspective." *Families and Television: A Book of Readings.* F. Brigham, Jr., and S. Preister, eds. Washington, D.C.: National Center for Family Studies at The Catholic University of America, 1987.

Vatican. *Charter of the Rights of the Family.* Washington, D.C.: USCC Office of Publishing and Promotion Services, 1983.

————, Congregation for Catholic Education. *Educational Guidance in Human Love: Outlines for Sex Education.* Washington, D.C.: USCC Office of Publishing and Promotion Services, 1983.

————, Congregation for the Doctrine of the Faith. *Instruction on Respect for Human Life in Its Origin and on the Dignity of Procreation: Replies to Certain Questions of the Day.* Washington, D.C.: Office of Publishing and Promotion Services, 1987

Voydanoff, P. "The Church and Economically Distressed Families." *Families, the Economy, and the Church: A Book of Readings and Discussion Guide.* F. Brigham, Jr., and S. Preister, eds. Washington, D.C.: USCC Office of Publishing and Promotion Services, 1987.

Walsh, F., ed. *Normal Family Process.* New York: Guilford Press, 1982.

Walters, T. P. *National Profile of Professional Religious Education Coordinators/Directors.* 1983.

Watzlawick, P., et al. *Pragmatics of Human Communication.* New York: W. W. Norton and Company, 1967.

Weiss, H. *Strengthening Families and Rebuilding the Social Infrastructure: A Review of Family Support and Education Programs.* A State-of-the-Art Paper Prepared for the Charles Stewart Mott Foundation. Flint, Michigan. 1983.

Weitzman, L. "The Economics of Divorce: Social and Economic Consequences of Property, Alimony and Child Support Awards." *UCLA Law Review* (August 1980).

————. *The Marriage Contract.* New York: Free Press, 1981.

Westhoff, C. F. "The Blending of Catholic Reproductive Behavior." *The Religious Dimension: New Directions in Quantitative Research.* New York: Academic Press, 1979.

————— and E. F. Jones. "The Secularization of U.S. Catholic Birth Control Practices." *Family Planning Perspectives* 9 (1977): 203-203.

Whitley, C. M. "The Sacrament of Marriage." *Homiletic and Pastoral Review* (April 1971): 34-42.

Wojtyla, K. *Fruitful and Responsible Love.* New York: Seabury Press, 1979.

—————. *Love and Responsibility.* English Edition. New York: Farrar, Straus and Girous, 1981.

Wrenn, M., ed. *Pope John Paul II and the Family.* Chicago: Franciscan Herald Press, 1983.

Yankelovich, D. *New Rules: Searching for Self-Fulfillment in a World Turned Upside Down.* New York: Random House, 1981.

Yorburg, B. *The Changing Family.* New York: Columbia University Press, 1972.

Young, J. J. "Current Positions on Divorce and Remarriage." *Remarriage* 1 (1): 3.

—————, ed. *Ministering to the Divorced Catholic.* New York: Paulist Press, 1979.

Zigler, E., H. Weiss and S. Kagan. *Programs to Strengthen Families.* New Haven, Conn.: Bush Center in Child Development and Social Policy, 1983.

Zimmerman, A. *Natural Family Planning: Nature's Way—God's Way.* Collegeville, Minn.: Human Life Center, 1980.

PRACTICAL RESOURCES FOR IMPLEMENTING A FAMILY PERSPECTIVE

This manual is concluded by directing persons interested in implementing a family perspective to resources still in preparation:

- *A Family Perspective Resource Book* will be developed by the writers of this manual as a companion to this volume. It will contain a practical tool for implementing a family perspective in parishes.
- The National Association of Catholic Diocesan Family Life Ministers has formed a committee to develop strategies and materials that will focus on implementation of a family perspective. The committee also encourages organizations, dioceses, parishes, and movements to develop their own practical tools to assist in incorporating a family perspective in their policies, programs, ministries, and services. If any organization, parish, or diocese develops a policy or a tool used for implementing a family perspective within their organization, please send a copy to the Bishops' Committee on Marriage and Family Life, National Conference of Catholic Bishops, 1312 Massachusetts Avenue. N.W., Washington, D.C. 20005.